More Praise for
*The Go-To Mom's Parents' Guide to Emotion Coaching
Young Children*

"Kimberley teaches us that paying attention to your child's emotions really matters, and she offers real-world examples for how to be a better parent. We could all use a Go-To Mom."
—Gary M. Blau, PhD; chief, Child, Adolescent and Family Branch, SAMHSA/Center for Mental Health Services

"Without Kimberley Clayton Blaine's developmental insights and her simple, straightforward discipline techniques, I would not be the parent I am today with an amazing relationship with my daughter. She has gifted us with a foundation to build upon for a lifetime."
—Susan Kay Wyatt, singer and songwriter,
The 12 Gifts of Birth Music

"Kimberley is the most trusted, savvy source of parenting wisdom."
—Amy Kovarick, author, *Baby on Board:
Becoming a Mother Without Losing Yourself*,
and radio host of *The Empowered Mother*

"The Go-To Mom provides a personal, readable resource for parents who want to emotion coach their children to become socially adept and compassionate. Within the context of relationships, parents are encouraged to attend to their children's feelings, look for the reasons for misbehavior, and guide their children to respond, without resorting to punishment or meaningless rewards as the means of discipline. The Go-To Mom's mantra of respect, love, and limits is manifested through vignettes and practical strategies to encourage a child's motivation to comply to age-appropriate behavioral expectations. Typical early childhood issues such as fears, tantrums, biting, sleep problems, shyness, potty training, and playground etiquette are addressed in a manner that inspires developmental progress and child well-being."

—Marie Kanne Poulsen, PhD; professor of pediatrics, USC Keck School of Medicine

THE GO-TO MOM'S PARENTS' GUIDE TO Emotion Coaching Young Children

THE GO-TO MOM'S
PARENTS' GUIDE TO
Emotion Coaching Young Children

Kimberley Clayton Blaine, MA, MFT

JOSSEY-BASS
A Wiley Imprint
www.josseybass.com

Published by Jossey-Bass
A Wiley Imprint
989 Market Street, San Francisco, CA 94103-1741—www.josseybass.com

Readers should be aware that Internet Web sites offered as citations and/or sources for further information may have changed or disappeared between the time this was written and when it is read.

Limit of Liability/Disclaimer of Warranty: While the publisher and author have used their best efforts in preparing this book, they make no representations or warranties with respect to the accuracy or completeness of the contents of this book and specifically disclaim any implied warranties of merchantability or fitness for a particular purpose. No warranty may be created or extended by sales representatives or written sales materials. The advice and strategies contained herein may not be suitable for your situation. You should consult with a professional where appropriate. Neither the publisher nor author shall be liable for any loss of profit or any other commercial damages, including but not limited to special, incidental, consequential, or other damages.

Jossey-Bass books and products are available through most bookstores. To contact Jossey-Bass directly call our Customer Care Department within the U.S. at 800-956-7739, outside the U.S. at 317-572-3986, or fax 317-572-4002.

Jossey-Bass also publishes its books in a variety of electronic formats. Some content that appears in print may not be available in electronic books.

Library of Congress Cataloging-in-Publication Data

Blaine, Kimberley Clayton, date.
The go-to mom's parents' guide to emotion coaching young children / Kimberley Clayton Blaine.
    p.   cm.
   Includes bibliographical references and index.
   ISBN 978-0-470-58497-2 (pbk.)
  1.   Emotions in children.   2.   Child rearing. 3.   Parent and child. 4.   Empathy. I. Title.
   BF723.E6B53 2010
   649'.64–dc22

                                      2010016269

Printed in the United States of America
FIRST EDITION
PB Printing 10 9 8 7 6 5 4 3 2 1

Dedicated to children everywhere—
who are entitled to grow up feeling
safe, loved, and worthwhile

With love and adoration
for my sons, Travis and Houston,
who someday will be amazing parents

CONTENTS

ACKNOWLEDGMENTS

A great deal of my time is spent alone, writing. Most of the people in my life know why I write and why I work. It has been a thrill to write this Go-To Mom's guide because it will allow me to contribute to the well-being of families with young children. I'm often asked if I ever get any sleep—I do, and a good amount. But sometimes I forget I'm working because I get so much out of it.

A special award must go to my supportive and sweet husband, Lee, for tolerating my love affair with my computer and TheGoToMom.TV. You're my knight in shining armor. It feels good to be loved.

My monkey-boys, Travis and Houston, are the light of my life, and without them I would have never become the Go-To Mom. I cherish the mornings they climb into our bed and snuggle with us.

My Sissy is truly my biggest and most dedicated fan. She was the lead mama in one of my first online shows! I would not be the confident Go-To Mom I am today if it wasn't for her insistence that everyone needs me.

Tracey Mallet introduced me to my literary agent, Linda Konner, and I was delighted when Linda decided to represent me.

It's an honor to be surrounded by people who believe in what I do. I've been blessed with the opportunity to work with the incredible team at Jossey-Bass who made this book a reality: Jennifer Wenzel, Erin Lane Bean, Nana Twumasi, and Michele Jones.

I was humbled, excited, and honored when I learned that Alan Rinzler was going to be my executive editor at Jossey-Bass. Thank you, Alan, for your guidance, expertise, and support.

Mary Emmons at Children's Institute has always allowed my creative energy to infiltrate the institute's early childhood programs so that I can continue to advocate for at-risk babies and toddlers.

My lifelong girlfriends have held my hand since I was twelve. Jackie and Sam Forrest, Susan McMartin, Jaime Bruce, and Dr. Diana Hoffman—I'm so lucky to have you with me on this journey.

Susan Kay Wyatt's positive energy constantly reminds me of the power of knowledge and how one person can touch so many lives. You are my soul-sista.

Being the Go-To Mom has opened many doors. When I'm not the Go-To Mom, I'm the Internet Mommy. Thank you, Beth Blecherman and Jill Asher for inviting me to write and produce for SiliconValleyMomsGroup.com. I cherish our friendship and partnerships.

Thank you to Jeanne Moeschler at Yahoo! for letting me play and be part of some truly exciting projects.

I'm thrilled to be a consultant and expert at the Pump Station in Los Angeles. Cheryl Petran, chief mom-nurturer, and Corkey Harvey and Wendy Haldeman, the cofounders, are leaders in the field of lactation support and have been dedicated supporters of the Go-To Mom.

Pat Forrest should be getting flowers sent to her once a year on my wedding anniversary. She set me up on a blind date with the man I married.

Thank you to everyone who's watched my Go-To Mom shows or followed me on Twitter and Facebook. When you value your role as a parent, you know how empowering it can be to have help at your fingertips.

THE GO-TO MOM'S PARENTS' GUIDE TO Emotion Coaching Young Children

Introduction

As the Go-To Mom, I work exclusively with parents, but early in my career I was the lead preschool teacher at the San Diego State's Infant and Child Study Center, where I spent years in charge of the four-year-olds' room.

Most people—parents included—can find a classroom full of preschool children quite overwhelming. It always came easy to me to deal with the challenging children who were most in need of guidance and attention. Soon it became routine for my coworkers to bring a "problem child" to my class instead of taking him or her to the preschool director's office.

Plenty of teachers claimed to listen to and hear what children said, but there was a lot of discounting and minimizing of kids' feelings as the teachers ran around trying to manage a class of lively children. I had a much better time than most with the so-called problem children, simply because I didn't demand an immediate change in their behavior. I wouldn't ridicule or shame them—instead, I acknowledged their experiences and difficulties and set firm limits. After observing and assessing them, I did my best to teach these children how to thrive emotionally, instead of punishing them for disruptive behavior. I was in the trenches, advocating for the feelings of every little boy and girl in that room. There wasn't a magical discipline style—it was my ability to create strong relationships that led children to cooperate. Back then, I *was* what is now known as an emotion coach; I just didn't know the proper term for it. Years later Dr. John Gottman officially coined the term *emotion coaching* in his important work with children.

During those early years of my career, I also worked as a group therapist, running a preschool-age group for Daughters and Sons United, a statewide program that provided therapy for sexually abused children. Finding myself with preschoolers day and night, I set out to learn all I could about this age group and its special needs.

Years later, as a licensed marriage and child therapist, I undertook a serious study of neuroscience and brain development. The literature confirmed that children learn best and are most receptive when raised in a nonpunitive environment. In terms of philosophy, I was aligned with the experts who advocated kindness and respect—peaceful parenting, if you will.

Around that time—in the mid-1990s—Daniel Goleman's groundbreaking book, *Emotional Intelligence*, was published. Goleman showed that fostering social and emotional intelligence was far more important than academic achievement for a child's happy, successful life. Successful people, we learned, had superior social skills and street smarts. Gottman wrote his own parenting book, *Raising an Emotionally Intelligent Child*. Ten years later, the idea of fostering emotional intelligence is a fairly well recognized concept among enlightened parents. What these parents look for are clear and concise strategies on how to incorporate this concept into their daily lives and discipline practices.

For years I coordinated child welfare and violence prevention trainings, working directly with abused children, and I became well versed with the current issues surrounding child abuse prevention and child welfare. I became the director of an in-home Parents as Teachers program and then moved on to directing national child abuse conferences. Shortly after this period, I opened my private practice in Los Angeles, married, and had my first baby.

At that point, my therapist hat flew out the window. Immediately I started relating more to moms and drifted away from training other professionals. I was now a mother, bringing all my hopes and dreams together with theoretical and practical experience to raising my own child. I decided to redirect my career from being treatment oriented, and focused more on the promotion of healthy children. It's my strong belief that if parents are equipped with high-quality child-rearing knowledge during the early years, incidents of child abuse can be reduced.

Today I'm the mother of two very active and challenging young boys. I do not and never have punished my sons; nor do I bribe, use sticker charts, or give time-outs. I work hard not to threaten or to remove privileges from them, but at times, when I'm emotionally charged, I know I'm not perfect and have to reevaluate my methods. I firmly believe that you don't have to overpower or bribe a child to get him or her to cooperate. The most powerful means of influencing behavior between any two people—and the heart of emotion coaching—is the strength of the relationship. However, this doesn't mean I don't set firm limits or use effective strategies to guide my boys toward making the best decisions. This book highlights invaluable tools on how to guide *your* child effectively through the most challenging years.

The good news is, emotion coaching is a humane and loving way of disciplining your child. Families and teachers I've worked with end up adopting this philosophy because it makes so much sense. It's logical and fits the human condition better than many outmoded theories of child rearing. Hitting, yelling, and threatening are things we don't even do to our pets, so why would anyone believe it's okay to do this to our children? Behavior charts, bribes, and rewards, though more benign, are not the answer either.

Quite often I'm amused by the responses I get from others who meet my kids. When friends or other parents meet my older boy, they often ask, "How do you have such a well-behaved child?"

My answer: "I don't. I just have the tools to honor him as a person, and in turn, he chooses to behave *most* of the time."

When they meet my younger son, who yells, hits, and consistently defies my husband and me, you can see them thinking, *How can a child development specialist parent a child like that?*

Here's the answer: because I have two boys who are completely different from each other, my strategies have to be uniquely appropriate for each of our sons. Regardless of their challenging behaviors, emotion coaching always keeps them connected to me.

With emotion coaching, I've effectively managed potty training, nightmares, picky eating, school phobias, the incredibly embarrassing supermarket tantrums, and challenging dining-out moments. Emotion coaching provides such a great example for my children that there's very little room for failure!

Emotion coaching means teaching your child from birth the importance and impact of her own emotions and how she can not only identify and label her feelings but also use these emotions to her benefit. Preverbal children have plenty of frustrations they are unable to communicate; emotion coaching allows parents to teach young children how to master their frustrations at a very early age. As children mature, emotion coaching allows them to feel accepted by their parents, to recognize and manage their own feelings, and to keep their impulses in check.

Emotion-coached children relate well to their peers; they play well with others and move easily from group to group. Ultimately, emotion coaching teaches children self-responsibility, and the benefits of this will last a lifetime. As a parent who emotion coaches, you'll give your children so much control over their lives from such a young age that when they enter the challenging waters of adolescence, they won't go off the deep end. We all know that the developing teenager is similar to the budding preschooler;

they're both looking for secure footing and experimenting with their newfound independence.

Becoming the Go-To Mom and launching my parenting video Web site has been the ideal culmination, combining all my years of professional experience with my own parenting knowledge. Having worked with thousands of children and their parents over the years, I've seen the amazing power of emotion coaching succeed countless times.

This book would not be complete if I didn't mention up front those who have taught me the value of standing up for the rights of children and have clearly influenced all my writings on early childhood and behavior: Haim Ginott, Adele Faber, Rudolf Dreikurs, Kathryn Kvols, Alfie Kohn, James Garbarino, Murray Strauss, Marshall Rosenberg, Ruth Beaglehole, John Gottman, Mary Emmons, and Bruce Perry.

I may not have solutions to every childhood problem, but I do hope what I say encourages you to rethink practices that don't honor children to their full potential. Just like other parents, I struggle to find the best remedies for the issues that challenge me in raising my kids; however, I do know it's good parenting to honor how children think and feel. Trust your instincts, and as you move forth with your children always ask yourself, *Is what I'm doing strengthening my relationship with my child, or is it potentially harmful in the long run?*

This book provides the tools, tips, and solutions that you need to emotion coach your child, as well as many real-life examples from clients and my own adventures in child rearing. I'm happy to offer these resources and guide you along the journey to raising a resilient, responsible, and fun-loving child.

Common Problems That Make Discipline Challenging

How Emotion Coaching Can Help

Children learn what they experience. They are like wet cement. Any word that falls on them makes an impact.

—Haim G. Ginott

I was raised in a household where there was very little tolerance for any emotion other than gratitude. Both my parents were highly driven entrepreneurs who focused their energies on keeping their businesses afloat. They gave little consideration to the fact that I was an extremely sensitive child, and as I grew up, I had no idea what to do with all my bottled-up feelings. It was difficult not being able to express all the anger, sadness, and uncertainty that I was holding in. I was afraid to tell people I had fears, so I hid them.

Back then I poured my frustrations into my journal. As an adult I came to terms with my emotions on my own. My temperament, interacting with my environment, led me to become a self-made expert on emotions. During my freshman year of college I worked in a preschool, where I began to feel a strong desire to help children in some way that went beyond a classroom setting. After college I started a graduate program in psychology and specialized in the treatment of traumatized children.

What stood out most in my academic and field research was that traumatized children usually lacked the ability to express themselves in the most basic way. Not only was self-expression a huge obstacle for them; just telling their story or describing their situation was often far beyond their capabilities. I found this among children of all ages. Traumatized children live in an environment where security and a sense of belonging are luxuries. Expressing emotions or having someone hear them out was not the norm.

What these children did have, however, was an acute ability to read their environment. They knew when danger was near and when to detach or protect themselves. What kind of world must that be, to have to take cover and never be able to describe or tell someone your personal experience?

It was easy for me to understand these kids because I'd been a child who was rarely heard. In junior high I was teased for being cold and withdrawn. My peers didn't know that it was my shy nature and internal fears that kept me from talking to others. It was difficult for me to engage with other people. At times I had trouble reading and writing. Trying to focus wasn't easy, and I was always preoccupied with my personal safety. I was sorely inept at identifying feelings and expressing my own internal world.

In the middle of my graduate internship, I was a court advocate on child abuse cases and had many favorable outcomes. I was the children's voice—often the only one. Some of the kids were only three years old. Gradually these children felt safe enough with me to begin their healing process. They began to verbalize their stories through emotion coaching.

It was then that I realized the power of emotion coaching, not only for children of trauma but for all children. Kids who aren't able to express themselves freely or who have fears around expression may grow up with issues that can prevent them from having healthy relationships and successful careers. Fostering emotional intelligence has become the basis for my work with families and young children.

WHAT IS EMOTION COACHING?

Emotion coaching is basically teaching your child emotion regulation—how to recognize and express various feelings appropriately. Through coaching, you help your child understand and communicate his feelings according to his developmental abilities.

Emotion coaching takes time and diligence—parenting in general requires both, so this shouldn't be surprising. You can emotion coach anywhere, but when feelings are running high, emotion coaching is most effective without an audience. Emotion coaching is particularly important when helping your child understand and express feelings that are overwhelming. I see emotion coaching as a way of life, not as a strategy you can apply to all misbehavior. Sometimes emotion coaching won't work, but if you can put in at least a 50 percent effort, the results will be favorable—and your relationship with your child will be stronger.

Your Role as Emotion Coach

Because you are your child's very first teacher and mentor, your role in the relationship is crucial. Families who emotion coach have clearly defined boundaries, and children in these families are more resilient, cooperative, and socially adept. You have more life experience than your child, which is to be expected—you've lived life much longer. Given your knowledge and experience, you're in the perfect position to be a wonderful role model and emotion coach.

The basis of emotion coaching is having you, the parent, help your child learn about feelings, relationships, social behavior, and the world around him. In order to be the best guide possible, though, you need to have a deep understanding of your child.

The Basic Elements of Emotion Coaching

The hallmark of emotion coaching is to permit your child to express herself emotionally without suppression or denial. In order to promote healthy communication between you and your child, you must

- Know and respect your child. Every child has his own personality, character, and temperament. This is not a one-size-fits-all approach.
- Know your child's developmental stage to avoid setting unrealistic or inappropriate expectations.
- Watch carefully for any emotions your child is trying to express and use challenging moments as a time to get to know your child better.
- Create an atmosphere of empathy and support for all of your child's emotions.
- Have a "power-with" relationship by sharing responsibility with your child, while setting limits.
- Encourage your child's internal motivation, rather than relying on external motivation (in other words, rewards) to change behavior.
- Model good behavior by thinking before you act.
- Avoid denying, discounting, or minimizing your child's feelings.
- Build your child's emotional vocabulary by listening to her and describing what you see.
- To encourage cooperation, prepare your child in advance as to what is expected.

Despite their good intentions, today's parents still rely on what is familiar and comfortable, which means they engage in some of the outdated parenting techniques used by their parents or in some cases in opposition to their parents.

Occasionally I encounter a parent who becomes defensive during the initial part of my parenting class. She has a hard time accessing her own feelings and says, "I can't emotion coach" or "I don't think it's a good idea to constantly tend to my child by always having to ask him how he feels." She has no idea how to deal with her child's heated emotions and thinks that emotion coaching may be coddling him or fueling the fire. I ask her to trust me, and disclose that I myself suffered from being raised in a home where emotional expression was forbidden.

As a child and as a young adult, I was at a disadvantage, and it took me well over twenty-five years to master healthy emotional balance. Luckily, in these modern times it is considered a regular part of child rearing for parents to address the myriad feelings they and their child experience.

I practice evidence-based parenting, which means that I use approaches that scientific and clinical studies have shown to have consistently positive outcomes, and I work closely with children. The various quick fixes and behavioral approaches you might see in magazines or on television, such as time-outs or removing of privileges, are not effective in the long run. Emotion coaching is dignified and gentle, and it works well. I say this as someone who has studied it extensively and subsequently practiced it with clients and my own children. My two boys have completely different temperaments from one another: one is calm and shy; the other is persistent and hyperactive. They require different initial approaches; however, I am consistently emotion coaching all along the way.

This chapter might be hard for some to read because we all have room for improvement as parents. I encourage you to stick with this book—read all the chapters and remember to give yourself a break, because parenting isn't easy. If you have difficulty addressing your own emotions, make it a priority to change—I'm living proof that a person can overcome her previous negative experiences with her emotions. I have faith that you too can grow and learn with your children the way I do with mine. I'm a passionate believer in emotion coaching because it ensures a successful outcome: cooperative, self-reliant, and responsible children. And isn't that every parent's goal?

COMMON OBSTACLES TO EMOTION COACHING

If emotion coaching is the answer, what stops every parent from doing it? I've come to recognize six common roadblocks that trip up the most well-meaning parents and make them ineffective when disciplining their children. Whether I'm at Disneyland, at the market, or just hanging out at the park with my kids, there's a common thread I see among most parents: they tend to rely on discipline styles that fall into one or more of the following categories.

Obstacle One: Control-Based or Hands-Off Parenting

Parents generally feel they have only two choices when misbehavior occurs: the first is control-based parenting, which is to punish the child because he's acting in a completely unacceptable manner. At the other extreme are hands-off parents. They're at their wits' end, so they just throw up their hands and give in, letting their child stay up late, skip the bath, eat what she pleases—whatever the issue may be. These parents aren't assertive and don't feel confident in setting limits or speaking firmly. They may believe that supervision is not necessary—that being their kid's best friend on a peer level is the best approach. Neither type of parent has any other, more effective tools at his or her disposal. Let's take an example:

The children are racing up and down the hallway, going back and forth—their feet pounding on the wood floor, their shrill voices piercing the air. Everything about this activity annoys the mom, who is trying to talk on the phone. The noise is becoming unbearable.

Control-based mom will throw down the phone, fling open the door, and scream, "STOP IT RIGHT NOW! YOU'RE DRIVING ME NUTS! Stop running in the hall and go to your room immediately! Now! Go play a game or something! Keep it up and there's no ice cream after dinner! You'll lose it!"

Let's keep in mind that what her kids are doing isn't dangerous, just hard on her nerves. The kids are young and full of energy, and they love to run, so what are they really doing wrong? Their spirits are high, they're excited; they certainly don't want to suddenly go sit down and play a board game. Making them go to their room is punishment. So is losing out on ice cream. Demands and threats are the reactions of a control-based parent.

Hands-off mom will simply sigh, shake her head, say to her friend, "Oh, it's just the usual craziness around here . . . so noisy . . . these kids are overtaking the house; what can you do?" and get off the phone, surrendering to the noise.

Neither the control-based or hands-off mom teaches her kids the skills necessary to respect the needs of others—something they'll have to have mastered by the time they enter school.

The middle road—accommodation through emotion coaching and setting limits—can give them the proper tools. In this particular case, there's no need for punishment, nor should the kids be allowed to disrupt their mother's phone call and peace of mind. Mom can choose to take another approach that is more appropriate for the developing child.

Emotion-coach mom would take a deep breath and say, "Guys, you're being super-loud. I see you have tons of energy—you're running like crazy chickens—can you take it outside, please? I can set up an obstacle course if you'd like; running is for outside. I'll come out and help as soon as I'm off the phone, but for now I need your help, so please head out back."

This solution is both effective and accommodating. We see that the emotion coach doesn't immediately scream, threaten, or punish.

Control-based and hands-off parenting can greatly hinder a child's ability to access and express emotions in acceptable ways. Neither approach allows kids to take responsibility for their actions. Control-based parents are the authoritarians with old-school beliefs, who think, "My child needs to listen and do what I say because I'm the parent. I'm the boss." Parents have all the say; they demand respect, and there's no sharing of control and teaching self-responsibility. This style of parenting is usually punitive and can involve threats, withholding love, and spanking. There's very little room for a child's self-expression or the acknowledging of a child's feelings.

Control-based parenting focuses only on behavior. We know that people are more than just their behavior—we're made up feelings, thoughts, opinions, and ideas. I've found that men in particular are more accustomed to control-based parenting because they're solution oriented. They want to fix any perceived problem quickly, and they tend to fall into the authoritarian role more easily than women. Women tend to be relationship oriented by nature, and they'll emotion coach without being aware they're doing it. Being solution oriented is a great trait to incorporate into parenting, but it's most helpful when a parent begins with emotion coaching.

However, when men are taught to emotion coach, they really enjoy both the process and the results. When I ask parents who employ the control-based approach how they feel about their parenting style, many say, "I do it because it's the only thing that works" or "My parents raised me that way; it worked for them, so it should work for me."

"If there were a different way that worked better," I ask, "would you do it?"

Invariably they say yes, because parents often feel bad about yelling or spanking; they just don't know another way that's effective.

"Do you want your child to fare better than you have in life?" I then ask, "Do you want them to reach the highest goals they're capable of?"

The answer is, of course, always yes.

My advice for these parents is to consider an alternative style that honors and encourages their children—because if the parents continue to use ineffective or harmful discipline measures, their children won't exceed the goals or meet their dreams.

Once fathers understand the end goal, they tend to make the connection and are open to emotion coaching. Emotion coaching is not about creating a bunch of wusses.

If I just recommend that control-based parents stop the threats, yelling, and punishments, most are not going to; they need to know *why* they should stop and to understand the concrete benefits of doing so. It greatly helps for you to step back and explore your own childhood and how you were raised, what you liked and didn't like as a child—with an emphasis on feelings, of course.

In the larger scheme, children are not going to become responsible when threatened, punished, or left to hang in the wind. All children need to be on the same social map when they grow up and leave their family to live their adult lives together in the community. Every child has a unique temperament. Some children are quite sensitive or shy. Others may be extroverted or persistent. It's important to find the middle ground and implement new ways of parenting, so that parents don't continue to resort to extreme and ineffective styles.

Words of Wisdom from a Parenting Expert

Do you want your children to listen to you because they fear you or because they love and respect you?

—Kathryn Kvols, *Redirecting Children's Behavior*

The overpowering parent and the hands-off parent often reap the same unfavorable end result from their child-rearing practices. Children who are raised in homes with controlling or coercive parents will always be looking for an opportunity to let loose, given their restrictive environments. When that opportunity comes along—usually when they're teenagers—they'll take it and run with it.

Children raised in households where "anything goes" lack boundaries and guidelines and have no idea where they fit in or belong. These kids are all over the place; they rarely experience containment and the secure attachment that's crucial for human development. They often feel scared because they lack the security of belonging in the family unit—Mom and Dad don't provide adequate structure. Down the road, many children of hands-off parents wind up in a situation similar to that of children of control-based parents: in some cases they have major boundary and relationship issues and are more frequently involved with drugs, gangs, and teen pregnancy because they're looking for a place to fit in and bond with others. Whatever is lacking at home, children will seek it out elsewhere.

The goal of emotion coaching is to give choices, provide empathy, and set limits, so when adolescence arrives, your child will say, "Drugs? I don't want drugs. My mom's making pizza tonight. I'm going home." If they're not getting love and guidance at home, kids will hunt for it somewhere else. If they're not there for your pizza, they'll go looking for a substitute, and might find it where people are cooking something they shouldn't be cooking.

Resilience Research

Everyone has the capacity for resilience. Resilience research shows that when the focus is on supporting and empowering children and youth, over 70 percent of young people in the most challenging of life conditions not only survive but grow into thriving adults.

—Sara Truebridge, MEd, WestED

Obstacle Two: Discounting, Minimizing, and Denying

It's an hour after her lunch, and the child says, "I'm hungry."

Mom answers dismissively, "You can't possibly be hungry! I just fed you an hour ago." This is an example of discounting the child's feelings. Discounting is the easiest, most knee-jerk response. Everyone does it, but that doesn't mean it's good or healthy for your child.

Imagine if an adult said the same thing. If Mom and her spouse went out to dinner and an hour later he turned to her and said, "I'm hungry," would she dismiss it out of hand and say, "No you're not. There's no way you could be"? Or would she say, "Didn't you get enough to eat at dinner? Did you have a hard workout today?" Most likely she'd ask and explore in a communicative manner and not completely dismiss his remark.

Emotion coaching is simply a matter of exploring instead of immediately discounting or denying a child's statement and feelings. Parents sometimes tend to put their own feelings and issues before their child's. Mom just ate, so she's not hungry; therefore her child can't possibly be either, and Mom may reply with "Oh, you couldn't be hungry" instead of saying something more supportive, such as, "You're hungry again? Really!? Is your stomach growling, or are you thirsty?"

When a child falls off a swing, the parent notices and thinks, *He fell right into some wood chips; how big a deal can it be?* and may say something like, "Come on, Aidan, get up; you're all right." This parent has good intentions—he wants to be sure his child isn't overly sensitive or a crybaby.

However, let's really think about the sensation a child has when he falls out of a swing. It brings up a whole slew of emotions. Surprise, for one thing: he was happily swinging and the next moment dumped hard on the ground. Embarrassment, for another: "Oh my gosh, everyone is looking at me! I look stupid . . ." The embarrassment might be worse than any real hurt Aidan suffers. Altogether, even a minor incident like falling off a swing brings up feelings that parents generally don't even know their child is experiencing.

Always Coming from a Position of Empathy As an emotion coach, you come from a place of empathy. Before jumping in to discount or minimize whatever just happened or was said, your first thought is always, *What is my child feeling?* The first step is to go over, check in with your child, and assess. "Hey, Aidan, are you all right?" You're simply affirming that you're there for him.

Half the time Aidan stands up, says "Yeah!" and gets back on the swing. That was easy; you're done.

But if Aidan is standing quietly, looking shaken, with tears in his eyes, you might ask, "Did you hurt yourself? Or are you just scared?" Aidan will probably answer with something like, "I got scared. I was up high and then I fell."

"Oh, yes, you were very high. It's scary to fall down. Do you want to come sit with me for a few minutes, then go back to the swings?" Be supportive without minimizing or denying. Such statements as, "Come on, get up, shake it off" don't help a child. You're only telling him that being hurt, scared, and embarrassed doesn't matter, that he needs to put up walls to appear strong. It may look okay for a child to do so; in fact, many parents praise children for this behavior: "Look at him—he got right up; good for him," but this reaction doesn't teach a child how to deal with uncomfortable feelings, which he'll need to handle later in life.

If parents respond empathically to their children's uncomfortable feelings, such as hurt, shame, guilt, or anger, they can teach their children how to process these feelings appropriately, giving them a skill they can carry with them into their adult relationships and the workplace.

"Do you like me? Do you love me? How much? Why haven't you called?" Everybody has had or known someone with an insecure boyfriend or girlfriend—the kind who calls several times a day and can never get enough reassurance. If these adults had been emotion coached as children, they wouldn't be acting and feeling so unsure of themselves now. Adults who've been emotion coached in childhood know where *they* end and where *others* begin—a very basic yet important boundary concept.

Guiding, Not Coddling When you emotion coach others, you assess the situation and deal with it. You're not coddling; you're shaping and guiding your child's emotional experience, whether she's feeling sadness, hunger, tiredness, or fear. The goal is to help children learn to keep their feelings in check while you also set appropriate boundaries.

I'm not advocating this sort of response every time a baby who's learning to walk falls down. In that case you simply let him get up and keep moving without your making a fuss; there's no need to intervene. The time for emotion coaching is when your child is crying or is in noticeable emotional distress. You don't discount or deny their feelings. Emotional distress means it's time to emotion coach, so your child knows he can count on you for unconditional support.

There are literally hundreds of everyday examples of discounting: "You're a big boy now. You should be able to walk all the way to the park. Come on, keep moving!" Or how about a parent who tells his frightened child, "Just jump in the pool. Don't worry: I'll catch you. JUMP NOW or we're done swimming!" and then rejects her because she doesn't jump.

When a young child is balking at your request, putting your own needs before hers by refusing to acknowledge that she's tired, fearful, or just worn out is a form of denying her emotional state.

True cooperation will eventually come when you accommodate your child's feelings and show him empathy. Here are some examples of helpful statements:

"Do you want Mom to hold you while we rest for a minute?"
"Maybe we need a juice break in the shade."
"Should we try this later?"

To keep pushing and pushing is disrespectful. It teaches your child that you're happy only when he complies with your requests.

Emotion coaching consistently while your children are young means you'll end up with children who don't need you as much, but in the best possible way! Constant denying or minimizing— "Come on, that didn't hurt, get up," "It's not that far, come on, keep walking"—will teach them that empathy is not important. They'll stop looking to you and expecting you (or others) to be there. You'll raise children who have difficulty empathizing with others.

When you raise children using judgmental statements, such as "Looks like that arm's broken. Come on, don't cry! Let's go to the doctor's . . . you're a tough guy, stop whining . . . ," they'll grow up and continue the harmful legacy of failing to teach empathy to their own children, perpetuating the negative pattern of self-centered, unempathic behavior. Children rely on adults to tend to them emotionally when they're in distress. Caring for our culture, society, and others starts in the home. What we do to our children, they will do to others.

Obstacle Three: Using External Motivation and Rewards

In my parenting groups, I'll ask moms and dads how they handle challenging moments or situations with their children, and I'd estimate that at least 70 percent describe a situation in which they use external or negative motivation.

A common one is, "I'm trying to potty-train my daughter, so I give her a sticker every time she goes in the little potty." Usually parents set up a system with a chart, and, after a week of earning stickers, the child receives a trip to the toy bucket or some other reward. This technique is an example of rewarding a child for a developmental process. Did you give her a sticker for walking? For talking? For being born? Then why give her stickers for controlling her bladder?

Yes, a child will sit on a potty and pee for a sticker, but if she does not yet have physiological bladder control and can't make it to the potty, she can't earn a sticker. In the amazing way that the brain copes, the child starts to tell herself, "I don't *want* a sticker or a prize!" She decides not to value the sticker or prize anymore!

Around this time the parent will tell me, "Well, the potty training worked great for a couple of weeks, but then . . ." The external factor or reward system they were using as motivation became ineffective.

Don't get me wrong—I love giving children stickers and prizes, but not when they're tied to controlling their behavior. No one is perfect, though, and you may find yourself deploying an "If you do this, I'll do that" tactic when you want your kid to do something. We all use the occasional prize or give a treat in an out-of-the-ordinary circumstance to get our kids to cooperate. Special treats or trinkets are fine for long road and airplane trips, as is something like giving a toddler popcorn while he sits in the stroller so that

Mom can try on shoes at the mall. That's fairly innocuous and really no big deal because it's keeping them occupied. However, the fact remains that asking your child to behave a certain way for a treat is manipulative.

Using behavior or reward charts should not become the basis of your parenting strategy. Using treats and stickers to coax normal cooperative behavior from your child is not a good routine. In school, in our careers, in life, we're all expected to be cooperative. It's our job as parents to guide and teach children the value of doing something without expecting to get something in return.

A Better Approach Children don't want stickers or a new toy; they want your attention. I enjoy giving presents, and sometimes I come home with the latest must-have toy (developmentally appropriate, of course!)—but not as a reward for my children's behavior. I don't believe in giving either of my sons toys to ensure compliance. My boys behave because we have a certain relationship. When they misbehave, it's usually because conditions are not good at that particular moment for whatever reason. A toy won't fix the problem. Something is amiss, and as a parent I need to recognize and address it.

Suppose you've just come home from a trip to the market. The car is loaded with cold groceries that need to be brought into the house, but your two-and-a-half-year-old is crying in frustration because she wants to play in your car. It would be an easy cop-out to say, "If you get out of the car now, Mommy will give you a cookie" (or, if she continues to resist, "If you don't get out of the car, you won't get to watch your show"). However, this is an opportunity to think beyond your immediate goal of refrigerating the perishables and to focus on a more important one, which is to teach your child the value of listening, cooperating, and doing the right thing. So instead of bribing, you can emotion coach and say, "I see you like to play in Mommy's car, and you're mad that Mommy won't let you stay. I'm sorry, baby. We have to go inside.

Can you help Mommy?" Then ask her to carry something in for you. Gently pick her up and go into the house. She'll still be upset, but chances are, this emotional burst will subside quickly because of your empathy. Your understanding and valuing of her ever-so-important little world will help her feel validated, and her anger will subside more quickly. If you bribe her, chances are that the next time she's playing in the car, she'll expect a treat in return for cooperation.

Obstacle Four: Using Negative Consequences as Punishment

Rewards and consequences must come in the proper context. This is where many parents become confused. I often hear, "We don't punish our children; we use consequences." My response is, "But are you doing it to make your child feel bad?"

"No," they reply, "we're doing it to teach them a lesson."

Let's get to the bottom of what teaching a lesson is really about. No matter what the context, the lesson is usually, "Now that you fear the consequences, are you ever going to do it again?" This stance has a negative impact on children. Kids thrive best when parents provide support, guidance, and solutions.

If your boss said something harsh to you to teach you a lesson—for example, "I told you to use Excel, not Word, you incompetent idiot!"—would you perform better? Or would you feel embarrassed and resentful? If, however, your boss calmly showed you a better way to complete the task, of course you'd do it—with pleasure and confidence, I'm sure. Negative consequences breed resentment, not accomplishment.

Four-year-old Peter takes the hose from his three-year-old sister, Jenny. Peter's mother asks him to give it back to her. Peter ignores her request, so Mom asks Peter to sit in a time-out. Mom feels that because Peter wasn't sharing and was ignoring her request, he should be given a consequence to teach him a lesson. But will placing Peter in time-out really help him understand the importance of sharing? What might work more successfully would be for the mom to say, "Peter, I see you wanted the hose, but Jenny was using it. Please give it back to her and ask her if you can use it when she's done." If he continues to ignore his mom's directive, she can ask him to sit with her and have a talk. Compared to administering a negative consequence such as a time-out, engaging in logical and reasonable conversations is much more effective for teaching children to share and make better choices. If Peter still can't control his grabbing, his mom can remove him from that activity until he's ready to share.

Using Natural Consequences Natural, not negative, consequences fit the context of the problem and are not intended to "teach a lesson" through punishment. Here is an example of how I emotion coached my son, then five; instead of focusing on "teaching him a lesson," I made sure that he shared responsibility for the consequences of his actions. When he went in the backyard to play, I reminded him, "If you choose to play ball and come in late for dinner, you'll still have to finish dinner at the regular time, and you might not have enough time left to eat dessert. Seven o'clock is dinner, and at seven-thirty you take your shower and have story time." Then I'd give him a five-minute warning to prep him and let him know when it would be seven o'clock, and at seven I'd call him in.

If he'd race in at ten minutes after seven, I wouldn't care. It was his choice and issue, not mine. If he started whining at seven-thirty, "But Mom, I want dessert," I'd say, "I know you do. I wish I could give you some, but dinnertime is over. What can you do differently tomorrow so don't miss your dessert time?"

I empathized about how it's a bummer to miss dessert because he loves to play outdoors; however, we also discussed that when he ignored my warnings and came in late, he pushed his dinnertime later. This is a natural consequence where dessert is directly related to the problem: his coming in late.

The consequence was not to punish him but to get him accustomed to responding to my first request to come inside. I'd remind him of our dinner and evening schedule and how important it was that we all eat at the same time so that we can all have dessert.

I didn't care if he played in the yard late every night and never got dessert, because I had given him autonomy and an opportunity to choose. There was no tug-of-war for control. I shared the responsibility and encouraged my son to think and to make decisions on his own. Clearly this type of scenario can't be expected of a toddler, but for a child who is five years or older, it works well.

I didn't withhold dessert from my son because I wanted him to be sad, but because he had to eventually learn to come inside when it was dinnertime. Dessert is directly related to our dinner and when we eat. An example of a consequence that is *not* natural would be if I were to say, "No TV tonight because you came in late for dinner." TV has nothing to do with being on time for dinner.

If my son cried, I felt bad, but I still wouldn't give him any dessert. I'd empathize and discuss solutions with him so that he wouldn't make a habit of being late for dinner.

"This really stinks," I'd say. "Let's make sure you get dessert tomorrow night. How can we be sure to get you inside for dinner on time?" I'd help him brainstorm solutions. This process is just the natural way of life for us because I'm not willing to engage in power struggles whenever things need to get done.

With *shared responsibility* instead of negative consequences, parents teach their children what to do *next time*—or at least brainstorm solutions with them. With emotion coaching, you empathize, talk about what went wrong, and neutralize all the negative feelings, then come up with a plan. The key to having cooperative children is to encourage them to be motivated internally. Children do things because they benefit personally from doing so, not because they're threatened or coerced.

AVOIDING NEGATIVE PARENTING

Emotion coaching means assessing and figuring out the motivation and feeling behind the child's behavior. When children misbehave, there's usually a reason: they have too much pent-up energy, or they're overexcited, not challenged, seeking attention, overtired . . . In many cases, the child's needs are not being met, but the parent does not correctly assess those needs and goes straight to employing punishment. Time-outs, spanking, berating, and withholding love are forms of punitive, negative motivation.

To motivate negatively means to do something hurtful or negative to a child with the hope that he'll then behave. Sending a child to sit in the corner of his room won't cause him to learn a lesson, because emotional pain doesn't produce positive results.

Still, parents continually add negativity to a child's experience, in hopes that their child will cooperate better. For example, Tasha keeps hitting the table during dinner at a café. Her mother sternly says, "Stop hitting the table. We don't hit the table during dinner!" Tasha stops for a few minutes, then, bang-bang-bang! She's hitting the table again, this time with both hands. Mom's next words: "Guess what, missy? You hit that table once more and it's time-out for you!"

Mom's message is, *You hit the table, I'll do something negative.* The threat of a time-out may deter her child from hitting the table, but the only thing Tasha's learning is obedience out of fear of her mother's anger or withdrawal of affection. We don't want our kids to learn that their only hope of getting their way or getting a need met is to comply with our demands and requirements.

If my child is banging on the table, my main goal is *not* to make him comply. I accept my child and his desires. I want to know *why* he's banging on the table. Maybe dinner is taking too long and he can't sit quietly any longer, or it's getting too late and he's overtired. Assess first—don't punish. Children don't absorb the messages we want them to learn when they're threatened.

Here's a more accommodating response:

Mom: Tasha, what's going on, sweetie? You're shaking the table. Do you have ants in your pants? Do we need to go take a walk and shake them out?

Tasha: No, Mommy, I don't want to take a walk. I'm bored.

Mom: I know it's hard to wait for dinner, but is it okay to bang on the table?

Tasha: No.

Mom: Why is it not okay to bang on the table?

Tasha: Things might spill, and break . . .

Mom: Yes, and then you'd have to wipe it all up. You don't want to have to do that, right?

Tasha: No.

Mom: No more banging. It's not okay. Would you like to draw? I have some pens. Or, if you need to take a walk, I'll get up with you. Just let me know.

Spanking

When you spank a child for poor behavior, you're likely to find that he'll repeat that behavior some other time because you didn't teach him the right thing to do or give him an alternative. Spanking doesn't teach a child what to do or what *not* to do; it teaches him only *Ow, ow, ow!* and that people with physical power always win. It's a quick fix, but is it worth the cost? Children who are hit are more likely, when they're adults, to continue the harmful legacy of spanking. In Chapter Four I go into detail on the detrimental long-term effects of spanking.

The same is true with sending a child to her room. Parents think they're teaching the child a lesson; meanwhile all the child is thinking is how mean Mommy is and what toy she's going to play with in her room—and what other type of parent she wishes she had instead of the one she's got.

When a child is raised with the practice of excessive control (both physical and emotional), his mind will develop to respond in either two ways: to ignore it, whereby the child becomes an expert in suppressing his feelings, or to process it by acting out. The child may act out in private, by hurting innocent beings, siblings, or family pets. Or, as an adult, he learns to control others.

We want children to grow up to be socially adept and to have compassion for others. Spanking, threatening, bribing, and rewarding are all short-term fixes. If you yell and hit, your child will yet and hit. Parents are their child's first and most influential role model. Honor your child, who may have different thoughts and feelings than you. Set boundaries and guidelines, but leave out the aggression.

The emotion-coaching parent views being a parent as something to be learned, and reads parenting books, attends parenting classes, or asks friends for advice when she faces challenges with her child. I have yet to meet a parent who actually likes to hit her child.

Holding Unrealistic Expectations

Here is a common situation I see: the parents are out for dinner with their two-year-old in a sit-down restaurant, and they're impatient because he won't behave. Let me tell you, it's just not going to happen—it's beyond the little one's capabilities! Parents need to bring toys and activities, engage the child in play at the table, entertain him, and take him outside for a walk a couple times. The bottom line is that parents need to accommodate young children, not the other way around, especially when a child's stage of development won't allow him to do what parents wish.

Parents who demand that their child sit still and behave at the table—constantly yelling "Stop it! I said *Stop it!*"—are behaving in direct contrast to the hands-off parents, who let their two-year-olds run wild in the aisles all over the restaurant. Both are classic examples of misguided expectations.

The parents in these situations have expectations that are either far too high or absent. No one should expect a two-year-old to sit through a sixty-minute meal; it's asking too much. Parents need to realize that they're only going to get possibly fifteen or twenty minutes at a restaurant, to accept that fact and be satisfied. It's actually fun to accommodate your child, because you always know what to expect. If, from the time you start to consider attending an event—let's say a concert in the park—you accept that your two-year-old won't make it all the way through, you'll go enjoy those first twenty minutes, hear as much as you can, then head for home. Life is much more enjoyable when you have realistic expectations.

Dad has high expectations of his four-year-old son, who hits his seventeen-month-old sister whenever she destroys his toys. Dad thinks his son should know better by now. Every time the son hits his little sister, he gets a time-out. We must naturally come to conclude that the time-outs aren't working because the boy is still hitting his sister.

Where does this punishment leave big brother? Probably feeling that he doesn't matter and that he can't and shouldn't express his frustration and anger. Young children are not proficient at emotion control, and when they feel overly frustrated, they may act out by hitting others. Although a four-year-old may look big, in reality he's not. Children need to be guided up until elementary school and beyond. The dad in this situation could acknowledge how hard it is to have a troublesome little sister, but can also set clear limits, by saying, "That's so annoying when she does that! Babies are hard to play around . . . but we never hit, ever. Use your words and come get me as soon as she messes with your toys. I'm here to help."

Potty training tends to be another area where a parent may have unrealistic expectations. If you have in your mind that your child will be potty trained by a certain age (which might lead to your resorting to bribes and rewards, pleading, and possibly even threats of punishment) and it doesn't happen according to your timetable, both you and your child will find it tremendously stressful. You're disappointed, and the child is ashamed.

This never-ending potty dilemma often causes a parent to stress out and constantly worry and check her child's pants. Don't set up an unrealistic timetable, because only your child knows how long her bladder can hold out. Let your child wear training pants or a pull-up. She'll get out of them on her own. I don't care if my sons choose to wear training pants until the eighth grade; I wouldn't mind a bit. Peer pressure will kick in and solve the problem. The reality is, children usually potty-train themselves when they're ready, which is typically by the time they're three years old, which we'll discuss in a later chapter.

If you impose your own issues and expectations on your child, parenting isn't much fun. Your child becomes anxious, and so do you. When you're realistic about things, it's not so hard to parent—and it's actually enjoyable!

Ignoring Your Child's Innate Temperament

If you know yourself and you know your child, things will go a lot more smoothly during challenging moments. The key is prevention. If you know your child has difficulties with transitions, for example, you can set up a strategy that takes this special need into account.

If your child is excitable around other children, you can encourage her to give other children their space and to come to you instead of pushing or hitting when her words aren't working. Working with your child's unique temperament sets him up for success. There will be fewer power struggles if you plant the seed of good behavior in a way that will get the best response.

Jill knows her daughter, Tiffany, is slow to warm up at play dates. At times she's embarrassed because Tiffany hides behind her legs for fifteen minutes before venturing off on her own. Because Mom is sensitive to this issue, she doesn't demand that Tiffany join her friends immediately—she knows that such pressure can potentially cause a meltdown. She prepares her daughter in advance by letting her know how hard it is to warm-up on a play date, but that she'll help Tiffany join the group if she'd like. Jill also tells her daughter that she'll be talking to other adults and won't be playing with her the entire time. This strategy accommodates Tiffany's temperament and slow-to-warm-up style, all in the hopes of avoiding unnecessary issues at the play date.

A one-size-fits-all response won't work with every challenging behavior. It's up to you to determine which approach will be most beneficial to you and your child. It may help you better understand your child if you're aware of how your own temperament drives your decisions and choices. You'll find peace of mind knowing that your child's temperament is truly half of the child-rearing puzzle. The other half is *how you* parent.

Children are an investment. All the effort we put into making sure that we're giving them the right tools to be healthy kids will pay off now and in the future. You can be there for your child by playing with her, offering support and empathy, asking questions, and, most important, listening to her. A strong parent-child relationship encourages children to be cooperative and good at playing with others—what great characteristics for growing into a healthy adult.

THE GO-TO MOM'S QUICK AND NIFTY TIPS

During times of discipline, ask yourself, *Am I ...*

Denying, discounting, or minimizing my child's feelings?

Punishing or giving a consequence to make my child feel bad?

Motivating through negativity?

Being too hard on myself as a parent?

If you answer yes to any of the above, restrategize and consider alternatives that give your child a sense of control and shared power.

The Importance of Emotion Coaching

> Parenthood is an endless series of small events,
> periodic conflicts, and sudden crises that call for a
> response. We would like to believe that only a
> disturbed parent responds in a way that is damaging
> to a child. Unfortunately, even parents who are
> loving and well meaning also blame, shame, accuse,
> ridicule, threaten, bribe, label, punish, preach and
> moralize.
>
> —Haim Ginott, *Between Parent and Child*

Colton's parents emotion coached him from the day he was born, always taking care to be open and accepting of all his emotions. He is a very mature four-year-old. One day Colton was at the park; he was with a group of other children who were engrossed in moving their push toys around in an endless circle. A toddler wandered into the group, and a couple of the boys rolled right over her feet with their toys. Zoom! The hurt toddler stood there in shock, then began to cry as the boys carried on, oblivious. The toddler's mom came rushing over.

Colton approached the little girl's mom and said, "I'm sorry my friends did that; they didn't even stop for her!"

The mom walked over to Colton's mother and said, "I'd like to talk to you; is that your son over there in the blue shirt?" she said as she pointed at Colton.

Colton's mom was surprised; she'd never had another parent approach her at the park before. *Guess there's always a first time,* she thought. "Yes; did he do something wrong?" she asked.

"I've never seen a child be so understanding. Your little boy came up to me and apologized for the other kids' behavior, and I want to thank you. I'm really impressed."

Emotion-coached children will do unto others what they want done unto them. When they see a friend has spilled his milk or broken a toy, they'll empathize. When Colton saw a baby in distress, he empathized the same way his parents would with him. I loved that Colton's parents got such early and public affirmation of the benefits of their coaching. They didn't have to wait until he was school age. They got feedback from someone in their community on their four-year-old son's ability to empathize.

WHY EMOTION COACH YOUR KIDS?

Being an emotion coach for your child will help her learn to recognize, express, and regulate her emotions. You'll be helping her with language development as well. Just think: fewer tantrums because your child will have the words to express her feelings rather than having to act out.

Emotion coaching promotes the deep connection between you and your child, strengthening your relationship and regular communication. With your guidance, your child learns valuable social skills and how to attend to the emotional cues of others. He'll learn to make new friends and will play well with others.

Emotion coaching helps your child build a "coat of armor" that protects her in times of adversity—she'll also recover more quickly from negative feelings and experiences. Emotion coaching helps your child learn patience and increases her ability to delay gratification and manage impulsive behaviors. Children who receive emotion coaching have better concentration at school and master learning tasks more easily.

Through emotion coaching, your child learns the value of connection, respect, and communication in relationships, so as an adult he'll be able to understand and support the emotions of others. With emotion coaching, you help your child become a compassionate parent when his time comes.

The mothers and fathers who come to my parenting groups want to learn new, positive discipline techniques because in many cases they're being challenged by their children's behavior and feel they have very few strategies that work. The goal of my parenting groups is to help parents raise resilient, cooperative children who are responsible and able to regulate their own emotions and impulses. In the class, parents learn new tools so that they no longer have to engage in endless power struggles or throw their hands in the air and give up. I also remind them how true success comes when both parent and child win.

BUILDING CONNECTION

The key to effective emotion coaching is *the strength of the relationship between you and your child.* It is the context for all your interactions. The four common obstacles discussed in the previous chapter involve parenting that is focused only on shaping behavior while neglecting or even harming the developing parent-child relationship.

Every interaction with your child provides you with an opportunity either to disconnect or to connect, to be overpowering or to share the power, to have all the responsibility or to teach responsibility. Before responding to your child, it's a good idea to ask yourself, *Will what I'm about to do help me connect with him and prepare him to make good choices both in the present and in the future?*

What Children Really Value Is Positive Time Spent with You!

A child who is treated like a mundane chore—fed, clothed, and routinely taken care of—doesn't necessarily feel loved. What makes children feel truly valued and worthwhile is one-on-one uninterrupted time with a parent. The average time a parent spends in conversation per day with his or her child is twelve minutes, and most of the child's interactions involve negative comments. This has to be changed. It's important to make efforts to spend more quality time with your children and to give them positive messages.

Children need guidance and support during their most challenging moments. When children get worked up, they can be very frustrating to deal with. However, if we react impulsively and become aggressive, then we put our relationship at risk. It takes only a few extra minutes to figure out what a child really needs. Planting the right seed—in other words, preparing your child in advance about what you expect—helps your child integrate and regulate certain emotions before they occur. And when your child has an emotional upheaval, it's helpful to acknowledge her emotional state. Ignoring it or minimizing it will only make her feel frustrated and misunderstood. Identifying and acknowledging feelings from your child's behavior can be trying, because you'll have your own reactions to the drama. But ignoring emotions only teaches children that self-expression is not important—which we know is not the case.

For instance, when Lola's upset because another child takes her toy, her mom, rather than chiding "You need to share, Lola. Let your friend have a turn!" could instead take a breath and say, "You look mad; do you need Mama's help?" By doing so, the mom helps Lola build her emotion vocabulary. She soon learns how to identify her own feelings as well as those of others. Lola also sees that Mom is supporting and guiding her, which strengthens their bond.

Acknowledging her feelings communicates that both she and her feelings are important and deserve her mother's time and attention. Lola will learn to depend on her feelings and begin to use them to her advantage through appropriate emotional expression. It's not worth the relationship strain to jump the gun and act impulsively by shutting your child down through lack of support. Taking time to guide your child is necessary in building your child's confidence and social emotional development.

The Importance of Playing with Your Child

Connection and closeness are crucial to a strong parent-child relationship! There are so many ways parents can connect to their children—and one of the best is through play. Play releases energy and provides opportunities to be involved in a child's world. Playing is how children process their inner feelings and work out their little-kid real-life issues. Parents who take the time to play with their children strengthen their understanding of their child's emotional world.

I like to play with my boys. It brings me closer in understanding their lives better and allows me to demonstrate appropriate sharing abilities. For example, my three-year-old takes my older son's toys. My older son gets very angry and yells at the little guy. I could intervene by blaming or ridiculing as a quick fix, or I can choose to connect to both boys and intervene such that everyone wins.

Boys: Give me that toy—ow! Stop it! Mommy, he's being mean!

Mom: Oh boy, I see everyone's upset here. It doesn't feel good to have someone take your toys without asking, does it?

Older son: No, it's mean.

Mom: Are there a few of these toys that your little brother can use? If not, I can take him out of the room; just let me know. *(Sitting with three-year-old now)* I see you like to play with things that big brother is using. He is playing with them. I know you're mad too! Maybe he'll let you use them later. Come with Mama; I have some pretzels and juice for your snack.

Older son: Okay, he can have two trucks, but only one of my trains . . .

A child who feels heard holds less resentment and is less oppositional. Giving children the right to express themselves allows them to feel valued, and a valued child wants to get along with others.

Offering Choices

While parents set conditions and limitations, they can also connect by offering their child choices whenever possible. Being allowed to make choices helps children become independent and accustomed to making decisions when parents are not present. Giving children a choice sends the message that you value their opinion, which increases their confidence.

Mom: Please put on your shoes. It's time to get in the car to go to Nana's.

Child: No. I'm not going to Nana's.

Mom: You look mad. Do you like home more than Nana's?

Child: Yes! I love my home.

Mom: Me too. I love our home.

Child: I'm staying here.

Mom: Can I stay with you? I wish I could stay home with you all week! But Nana will miss you, and my work will miss me!

Child: No shoes.

Mom: I can help you with your shoes, or you can put them on yourself. (*gives child plenty of time to think*)

Child (huffing and puffing, trying to keep some control): YOU.

Mom: Thank you for helping Mama out. Can you make me a picture today at Nana's house? What is your favorite paint color to use?

Instead of making threats or rejecting your child during challenging moments, you can use this as a time to bond and get to know him better. Learning emotion regulation is a slowly evolving process for children, and they depend on you to coach them through various unpleasant feelings.

THE POWER OF EMPATHY

At the heart of everything I teach, and the foundation for successful emotion coaching, is *empathy*. Empathy is quite simple: it's the ability to feel what your child is feeling. To emotion coach your child is to put yourself in her shoes and respond accordingly.

Setting Aside Your Own Emotions

Probably the hardest part of empathy is setting aside your own emotions and reactions in order to understand those of your child. How you understand, experience, and express your feelings will definitely have an impact on how you understand those of others. Culture, gender, and your family history all played a role in how you learned to deal with your feelings.

Empathy is a very powerful tool, particularly when your child is experiencing negative feelings. For instance, when your child gets angry with you for keeping him inside because it's too hot outside, you can be sure he'll let you know. Your most empathic response would be to set aside your frustration with the situation and say, "It makes you mad when Daddy doesn't take you outside to play. That must be hard for you. I'm sorry. Would you like to play a game?"

Again, you're sending the message that your child has a right to be angry. More important, by identifying the feeling so that he can continue to develop his emotion vocabulary, you're communicating that anger is just another feeling we can manage.

By empathizing with a child's feelings in a specific situation, you enable any negative reaction to pass sooner than if you respond with distraction techniques or by discounting by saying something like "Oh, come on, you play outside all the time. You don't need to be upset; we have plenty to do inside." Both of these responses will only make your child angrier or will make him doubt his own feelings.

The Everyday Practice of Empathy

The other night my older son fussed while taking a shower and was really whining loudly. It had been a long day, and I was still trying to do a hundred things at once. My nerves were shot. I marched down the hall to the bathroom and yanked open the shower door. There stood my son, sad and exhausted, howling "Mommy, Mommy . . ."

What I wanted to blurt out was, "Stop the whining—now! I'm busy trying to fix dinner. Finish in the shower and speak in a regular voice." However, that would have been fighting for control, which I didn't want to do, and by giving into this impulse I would only have escalated the tension and created more trouble.

As I opened the shower door, I caught a glimpse of the pink Go-To Mom empathy reminder bracelet I wear on my wrist. The bracelet is stamped EMPATHY, to remind me of the most important value for my children every minute of every day of our lives. It reminded me to calm down and empathize. I took a deep breath and consciously decided to take an extra minute to emotion coach:

> *Mom:* Honey, you look really tired. Are you tired out?
> *Son:* Yesssss . . . Mommy, will you wash me?
> *Mom:* I know you like it when Mommy washes you, especially on nights like this when you're so tired, but I have to finish making dinner. Please wash up, because I can't stay here with you. I'm sorry you're so tired, but you're dirty. Wash up and then come eat, sweetie.
> *Son:* Okay.

Returning to the kitchen, I was thankful I'd been reminded once again of the power of empathy. No one's a perfect parent—that's why I created the empathy bracelet, because even I need to be reminded to stop, think, and respond empathically during difficult moments with my kids.

UNDERSTANDING YOUR CHILD'S TEMPERAMENT

There are several other important factors to keep in mind as you prepare to emotion coach. The first is to recognize and know your child's temperament and her normal behavior. Some children are naturally more boisterous and free-spirited than those with shyer, more withdrawn personalities; actions that would be cause for concern in one sibling may be typical in another. As the parent, you're the best judge of your child's typical demeanor and behavior and can adjust your emotion-coaching style accordingly.

My older child is very focused and is good at taking direction. Giving him a five-minute warning when it's time to clean up works well. However, my energetic and outgoing three-year-old is a different story. He doesn't hear warnings. He needs me to walk over and place my hand on his back and speak closely to him. His focus is scattered, so I'm always close to him when I give a warning to clean up. If either son rebels or is disgruntled, I still remain the emotion coach while setting expectations and limits.

Successful emotion coaching also means acknowledging your own relationship with feelings. Simply becoming aware that certain situations seem to anger you helps you prepare for them so that your own emotions don't get in the way of coaching.

BEING AWARE OF DEVELOPMENTAL STAGES

Knowing your child's developmental stage is also a vital element of emotion coaching; it enables you to avoid setting unrealistic or "out of whack" expectations. With this key element in place, you're ready to emotion coach!

If your child is two years old or younger, redirecting is usually the most effective tactic. For example, if it's too hot to play outdoors and your child is upset, you can acknowledge and empathize with her feelings first, then redirect her attention.

To redirect, you might say, "It's hard to stay inside when you love to play in the yard. We are staying inside right now. Let's go find your stick pony. Look, he's right here!" You might also ask if there's another special toy or book she can play with. This gets her accustomed to brainstorming for solutions.

One of my "hot buttons" is pushed when my younger son runs away from me. This irks me to no end! My older son has always been a pretty good listener and talks with me if he disagrees with one of my requests. However, my daredevil little guy races around the house whenever it's time for a bath or dinner.

It helps me to recognize that my little one is not going to comply just because I'm a licensed child therapist, and that he's just engaging in the normal crazy antics that kids of his age often go through. No matter how frustrated I get, I take a break and refrain from yelling across the room, "Get over here now!" I matter-of-factly inform him that when he's done running around, he has to help me. I acknowledge that he loves to be chased, then ask how much time he needs. He usually says, "One big minute." After his whirlwind of racing, I give him a warning: "I will come and pick you up, or you can walk to the bath." Two choices and that's it. Most of the time he walks; the other times I carry him or guide him with a gentle touch.

As your child gets older, you can encourage her to come up with ways to solve her frustrations or challenges: "Since we can't play outside right now, what are some ideas of what you can do instead?" If she responds to your question with "Nothing. There's nothing fun to do in here," take this as a good opportunity to empathize and give her some time. You might say, "I see you're still upset. When you're feeling ready to figure out what to do, let me know." If she asks for help, you can offer some ideas, but let her find some for herself as well. You're honoring her feelings and letting her know that you won't abandon her when she expresses herself. You're right there—even when she's angry or upset—which keeps you connected.

KEY STEPS OF EMOTION COACHING

With practice and diligence, emotion coaching will become second nature. Let's go back to Colton—the compassionate little boy at the park. What, exactly, did Colton's parents do to make him aware of how others feel? They followed the steps here as a natural part of raising Colton.

Planting the Seed

Planting the seed means preparing ahead of time by helping your child understand what to expect in certain situations and what will be expected of him. When expectations are clearly laid out, children are far more likely to cooperate and less likely to be disruptive.

When my husband and I plan to take our children out to dinner, I bring the subject up early in the day. I say to our boys, "We're going to a restaurant for dinner tonight. What does that mean? It means that we're all going to sit together in the booth and eat our food at the table. No yelling and no running around." That's it; a simple statement preparing them for the event, including what they *can* and *cannot* do at the restaurant. We pack an activity bag with lots of fun things to do at the table.

As we drive to the restaurant, I give my children a reminder. "We're on the way to dinner. That means we're going to eat at the table and sit in the booth quietly. No running around, no yelling."

I remind my younger son as we enter, "We're going into the restaurant to eat our dinner. Remember what we talked about?" As soon as we're seated, we make a remark to the effect of, "Isn't this great? We're going to have such a nice meal." We hand each child a toy and interact with both to keep them occupied. Isn't the whole idea of going out for dinner to have fun? We make the experience as enjoyable as possible for our children, and accommodate them when necessary, but most important, we had made sure to *plant the seed* for cooperative behavior.

Assessing and Observing

Assessing and observing simply means paying attention. Monitor your child's behavior—when is he most likely to become upset, cranky, or frustrated? What is your child's basic temperament? What situations are most upsetting to your child? The triggers for such feelings change as your child grows older. What frustrates him at age two will no longer frustrate him at four, because he'll have developed more sophisticated coping skills and achieved a higher level of tolerance.

If you know that a certain toy frustrates your child, be sure to sit with her while she attempts to play with it. Observe her attempts to figure it out and offer help when she seeks it. Instead of giving her the answers or fixing the problem for her, provide guidance by helping her learn strategies to master her skills. Demonstrate, but give her the opportunity to do it herself. Observing your child and knowing her triggers will help you predict when challenging situations will arise and prepare your child for them.

Part of observing also means assessing your child's needs. Is he hungry, thirsty, tired, too hot, too cold, or overstimulated? Problematic behavior is often simply your child's expression of one of these basic needs. Meeting his need will quickly stop the meltdown.

Listening

We all want to believe that we listen carefully to what our children are saying. Listening certainly sounds easy enough, and no one doubts its importance, but as I learned when I worked at a busy preschool, many adults claim they're listening while their attention is much too scattered to really hear what a child is saying.

This is certainly true for many overstressed parents. Children are remarkably patient when you're doing your best to understand and listen with undivided attention. But, fortunately, your child will absolutely let you know when you're distracted or not being a good listener.

> Son (*reading his book*): Can you look at this, Mom? This is not a king; it's a prince.
> Mom (*doing dishes*): Yes, it's a king.
> Son: Aw, you're not listening. Forget it.
> Mom: I'm right next to you—I'm listening, honey.
> Son: I know you're here, but I feel you're not.

Listening skills are crucial to emotion coaching. Listening to your young child is different than listening to adults. You need to pay attention both with your eyes *and* with your ears. This may even take getting down on your knees to be at his level and looking directly into his eyes so he's sure he has your undivided attention. Good listening requires not only paying attention to the words your child is saying but also watching his body language.

I like to keep this mantra in mind from Adele Faber and Elaine Mazlish's groundbreaking book *How to Talk So Kids Will Listen and Listen So Kids Will Talk*: "Listen first, talk second."

Identifying and Acknowledging Feelings

When your child is in a situation that causes her to feel a strong emotional reaction, or when she is misbehaving, you help her most by recognizing and responding to the feelings she is expressing. Identifying and acknowledging emotions that your child is expressing through misbehavior can be a little more difficult because, as I've mentioned, you will probably have your own emotional reactions to what she is doing. In any case, your job as an emotion coach is to help your child understand what she is experiencing.

For instance, when your child is red-faced and crying because another child has shouted mean words at him, you can deal with the situation in one of two ways: you can be dismissive of his feelings, immediately trying to diffuse the situation by convincing your child to ignore what happened; or you can validate his experience by commenting on the emotion you see: "You look really mad right now. Do you need Dada's help?" By doing so, you help him build his emotion vocabulary. He soon learns that this feeling inside is called *mad*. He also learns that this is what people look like when they are angry, so he will learn how to read the emotions of others and appropriately deal with his own. Encourage him to tell the other child how he feels. Never allow your child to physically lash out at another. Only encourage self-expression and show him how it's done.

Empathizing

Empathy is a powerful tool, particularly when your child is experiencing negative feelings. His feeling will pass sooner if you respond by putting yourself in his shoes rather than coming back at him with a minimizing statement or an attempt at distraction. When I feel understood, I'm less likely to become defensive and have less of a need to withdraw from others. Children are no different than adults: we all feel comforted when we are heard and understood by someone who cares about us.

OTHER THINGS TO KEEP IN MIND WHILE EMOTION COACHING

In a nutshell, emotion-coached kids know how important and powerful all emotions can be. These kids grow up stronger and more confident in their ability to communicate when you're mindful and available to them.

Keep Body and Mind Connected

One of the key things to keep in mind about emotion coaching is matching your body language with your words. If you sigh in a very put-upon way and snap, "It's fine," while you're angrily mopping up spilled milk, your body language and tone are clearly not matching your words. Children recognize the disconnect between what you say and how you act, and become confused. To emotion coach effectively, your body and mind must be on the same page.

My older son is socially conscious and very adept at recognizing the emotions of others. I walked into the kitchen after having a mild disagreement with my husband. My son asked me, "Mommy, are you happy?" I said, "Yes sweetie, I'm happy," and continued to try to hide my annoyance about my heated exchange with my hubby. My son then said, "You don't look or act happy." Emotion-coached kids are experts at reading verbal and nonverbal cues.

Let Your Child Know Grown-Ups Are Here to Help

Teaching young kids the word "help" can reduce a lot of screaming and whining. For young children who don't yet have the necessary words to get what they want, screaming is the best way to get the attention of those who can help. By teaching your toddler the word "help," she'll replace the screaming with the new word.

As your child grows, sometimes he won't know who can help with a specific situation. Be sure to let him know that you and other grown-ups are here for him. "Mommy is here to help; I will always help you." Reminding him that you're here to assist teaches your child to come to you when in need. Children tend to be aggressive when they have a limited vocabulary, so this is useful in encouraging children to use their "words" instead of their hands—and to come get a grown up when in need.

To help your child build her emotion vocabulary, you need to be consistent when she asks for help. Remember to engage your skills. Observe, listen, identify feelings, use the word "help," and then follow through with helping. These tricky emotional moments are times to bond and connect!

There's nothing more satisfying to a child than to have her loved one understand and help her when emotions run high. Doing so strengthens your connection and relationship. The more consistently you help, either with a task or through emotion coaching, the more your child will trust that you're a reliable ally, and she'll better understand how to use the skills you're teaching. She'll learn to do what you do because she constantly watches and learns from *you*.

PRACTICING EMOTION COACHING

Emotion coaching becomes easier with time and practice. The first three elements—planting the seed, assessing and observing, and listening—will soon be second nature. You'll be able to better acknowledge feelings, empathize, and brainstorm as problem-solving tools. As with everything else, practice makes perfect as you strive toward consistently being the best emotion coach you can be!

Jose Coaches His Resistant Daughter

Jose has a four-year-old daughter, Mari, who is going through a very defiant stage. Her answer to all her parents' requests is, "Not now. Not now." A three-year-old will just say no, but at four years of age, children rapidly gain independence and become more advanced in their refusals. Jose explained to our group, "When my daughter talks back, I feel she needs a consequence—I'm her father! She should do what I tell her, right?"

I empathized with Jose that nobody likes it when a child talks back or downright refuses a request. I encouraged him to think of some alternatives to try based on the idea of shared responsibility, which means that the parent is empathic while setting firm limits so that the child knows what is expected and how she should follow through. Sometimes it's a challenge to set firm limits while being supportive, but we encouraged Jose to make the attempt.

At our next weekly group, I asked Jose, "What was your issue last night?"

"Mari refused to take her bath again. Absolutely refused. No, no, no, is all she would say. I offered her toys, I showed her what fun it would be; nothing helped. She still didn't listen when I told her she'd have no story if she didn't get in. When I finally just picked her up and took her in, she screamed and screamed."

We discussed ways to eliminate the power struggle.

Practicing Planting the Seed Prevention is the key. Jose should start *planting the seed* well before bath time. At the playground he can say, "Mari, bath time is after dinner tonight. Are you going to help me out by getting into the tub when I ask you to?" This is always the first step to preventing struggle. Reminders lead to less resistance.

Perhaps she's steadfast against taking a bath, feeling defiant or merely asking, "Why can't I go to bed dirty?"

Jose can explain, "We keep ourselves clean to stay healthy; that's why there are showers and baths. When we go out and play, we get dirty; that's why we take baths and showers." Jose should leave the explanation at that, but he has *listened* to his daughter and answered her question.

This is also a good time to *empathize*. Jose can say to Mari, "I know that sometimes it's fun to be really dirty—like when we go camping and get dirty from hiking. That's fun, but we don't do that every day. Tonight you need to take a bath."

Practicing Assessing and Observing That evening, Jose will *assess and observe*. Mari is happily playing with her Polly Pocket doll and doesn't want to stop. There's definitely going to be some resistance. Jose can plant the seed and empathize, but in the end he's only going to offer two choices, because Mari needs to have a bath. Giving kids a choice makes them feel that they have some power or some say in the matter. For example, Jose can ask Mari if she'd like to bathe with toys or without toys. On the nights she is dirty, there is a bath time; Jose will remain consistent on that point. What he can offer is an empathic ear, two choices, or an opportunity to brainstorm.

> Jose: It's tough to stop playing and take a bath when you're having such a good time. No one wants to stop having fun. I know washing can be a chore sometimes. We need to get you clean because we can't let you go to bed with a dirty body. Mari, what can we do?

Mari: I don't know. I want to play with Polly. Don't wanna bath.

Jose: Right now it is your bath time, like we talked about today, so we need to go. Maybe Polly Pocket could come with us and watch you take your bath.

Mari: No, Daddy, Polly's happy in her house. She doesn't want to watch a bath.

Jose: I see. Polly likes her house, but where's her bathtub? I don't see one.

Mari: She doesn't have one, and if I have to take a bath, Polly does too!

Jose: We could probably make her a bath. What could we use to make her a tub? Hey! How about a cup? Let's put Polly in a cup while you're in the tub, and afterward we'll build her a real tub of her own. (*Jose is helping Mari brainstorm for solutions.*)

Mari: Yes, a cup! (*said as she happily trots to the bathtub*)

Respect gets children motivated more than anything else. Jose didn't just tell his daughter what to do while she was playing—he offered her some control so that they were no longer fighting for it. He avoided getting into a tug-of-war with his four-year-old. He empathized and offered options while setting limits, and she understood, responding without the dreaded power struggle.

FESS UP WHEN YOU SLIP UP

You not only teach your child through emotion coaching but also serve as a role model. As you show empathy, your child learns to become empathic. By your labeling and talking about emotions, your child learns that emotions are manageable, and he will feel comfortable expressing them in an appropriate manner. Eventually he will be able to coach himself and brainstorm to find solutions to his problems.

In the course of your "career" as a role model, however, you'll need to remember that you're a human being first and a parent second, so you can expect an occasional slip back into old, ineffective responses. The goal is to catch yourself and then repair the connection with your child. Your mistakes and shortcomings can thus themselves serve as wonderful opportunities for you to be a good role model. In such situations, "fessing up" can be particularly powerful. Fessing up means that you genuinely apologize to your child for making a mistake. When fessing up, be specific, identify the behaviors for which you are apologizing, and share the feelings you were experiencing at the time and how you felt afterwards. You're demonstrating that you're not perfect and that it's okay.

You show your child that it's all right not to be perfect. We all make mistakes every now and then, and fessing up is a natural and healthy way to prepare your child for the imperfections in the world and to help him establish and maintain relationships.

Personally, I slip plenty of times! When I'm particularly busy and stressed out, I may fall into saying, "I said *now!*"—but I immediately follow up with, "I'm sorry I used that tone of voice, but Mommy is hot and tired, and I only use that voice when I'm at my wits' end. I'm trying to get us out the door on time and need some help. Can you please help?"

If you find yourself too overwhelmed to emotion coach, it's important to let your child know that even parents make mistakes and that you feel bad about your inappropriate response. The great thing about children is that they're innately compassionate and forgiving. They'll do their best to help out. Children don't empathize with parents who are punishers, but if you're an emotion coach, they'll empathize with you when you are having a hard time and you fall back into old patterns. Whatever you give, you will more than get back.

In fact, the time may come when your child emotionally and socially outgrows you! They'll see situations clearly, because you've taught them to be sensitive to others and to themselves. Children who've been emotion coached learn to identify what's right and wrong—hence they become more efficient in reading the cues of others. When you do something wrong, they'll know it immediately and call you on it. Emotion-coached children help parents when they fall off the emotional wagon! My sons have called me on my behavior more than once—and I don't mind saying that I'm an authentic mother with imperfections. It surely keeps me on my toes!

THE GO-TO MOM'S
QUICK AND NIFTY TIPS

When your child is in the midst of emotional upheaval, your first impulse may be to offer solutions or set limits; however, it is during these most heated times that you should do nothing but empathize. Once everyone is calm, then you and your child can explore solutions together. The bonding that occurs while you are empathizing with your child is an amazing experience, and is the number one tool that I encourage families to use.

3

Baby Discipline

Is There Such a Thing?

. . . our children perch on the edge of their nest.
They flap their wings, squawk, and arch their necks
at us. . . . The challenge is to realize that each flap is
an opportunity. Every squawk a message. Each arch
is a gift.

—Mary Sheedy Kurcinka

Parents typically spend the first year of their baby's life trying to get to the next stage of development. Alan Schore, a professor at UCLA's Department of Psychiatry and Biobehavioral Sciences, describes this parent-child interaction as the *excitatory phase*—during which we try to bring baby out of her shell by encouraging her to explore, talk, and interact. We coo, hold her in a standing position, or try to see if she'll reach for a toy. We're intent on progress and encourage all the increasing number of skills that come with our baby's development.

Parents typically spend the second year of their baby's life keeping baby out of danger by protecting her and being hypervigilant about supervision. This is when the excitatory phase ends and the *inhibitory phase* begins. Babies learn to venture out, crawl, then eventually walk and run. Parents follow baby and tell her *Don't touch, Watch out, Don't go there, Not for baby!* Because you are more verbally directive with your baby while she's exploring, you can naturally begin emotion coaching at this phase, which is around her first birthday.

BEGINNING TO INFLUENCE DEVELOPMENT

Everything you do during the first two years of life with your baby will influence and determine his development—both now and in the future. This is the most critical time for bonding and attachment to occur. When you pick up your crying baby, she knows you're there for her. When you rock, cuddle, and hold her before she sleeps, she learns that sleeping is safe and peaceful. Tending to her when she is in distress or frustrated teaches her she's valued and worth your time and attention. When you love and cherish her, she will learn to love others.

Your behavior during these years shapes and influences many important neural connections in your baby's brain that will either be beneficial or detrimental to her development; this is what Bruce Perry calls the *use it or lose it* concept. A child who is not touched, held, or spoken to will not attach or appropriately respond to people in his life. When he grows up he will be ill-equipped to maintain meaningful and healthy relationships. Young children depend on their parents to guide them along the way through early childhood. You have the first two years of life to do it right.

How Babies Learn

Baby brains have many more neural connections than adult brains. But they are much less efficient. As your baby's brain grows, the connections that are not used die out, and the remaining ones become hardwired and automatic. The brain will practice what it's taught. When children are raised in a hostile, chaotic household, they'll develop and be most competent in the behaviors that help them adapt to that situation. Conversely, if a child is raised in a home with little or no interaction, they won't learn the necessary social coping skills to function as an adult. If we expose children to loving, calm, and safe environments, they'll learn to respond by developing and sharpening those traits in themselves.

Neurologically, their brain will be influenced by everything you do. Of course your baby is born with all the cells, neurons, and synapses she needs to be capable of learning. The brain is still growing, however, and depends partially on the environment to shape it. Early childhood is a fragile time for brain development, and negative or harmful experiences can't be easily undone. You can still influence your child's brain development and his experiences later in his life, so don't get discouraged—I'm just pointing out that the most crucial time for your child is when the window for healthy attachment is open.

If you have that much power and influence, wouldn't you want the best for your baby? Use it or lose it. Simple. Expose your baby to healthy caregiving, teach appropriate and tolerant self-expression, and most important, love your child unconditionally.

There Is No Such Thing as Spoiling a New Baby

Babies have no language or easy ways of telling us what they need. Babies cry as a way to communicate their needs. All we can do is read their body language (smiles, frowns, cries, rubbing of tired eyes . . .) and become an expert at interpreting all their cues.

With such limited brain development, babies who are six months old or younger are incapable of manipulative behavior and have very limited ability to self-soothe—hence the heavy reliance on caregivers. Research shows that babies who are held and comforted actually cry less, learn to trust, and are more independent.

Tune in to your baby's reactions and responses, learning her individual cues that let you know when she needs to be alone or have quiet time. It's possible to overstimulate a baby with too much talking, touching, and singing. For instance, some babies might look away, cough, or become irritable to let us know when they've had enough handling and playing.

Give yourself permission to love, rock, cradle, and hold your baby when your instincts tell you to—and give yourself permission to let your child rest and enjoy calming, quiet time as well.

What About Crying It Out?

The amount of information out there on the controversy of letting your baby "cry it out" can make you dizzy and confused. That's because as parents we're innately programmed not to let our babies suffer. Letting a baby cry it out is by far harder on the parents than on the baby.

I don't recommend letting a newborn cry it out. I believe that because babies have an immature nervous system, for at least the first four months of life they need to be held and rocked when they cry.

Many experts and parents believe that babies need to learn to fall asleep on their own to develop good sleeping habits. I don't disagree with that. Babies certainly need to adapt to sleep. However, I do think that a child who is under six months of age still needs her parents to soothe and comfort her as a part of learning to fall asleep peacefully and securely.

We moms know the emotional pain of letting our baby cry it out. It tears at our hearts and makes us feel like a bad mommy. I felt more comfortable letting my babies cry a little at night to fall asleep once they had good muscle control in their tummy and were able to sit up in their crib—which for them was at around the six-month mark. I knew that with this new mobility they were safe. It also helped to have a mini video monitor to observe them and know when I was needed.

A parent can learn the difference between a tired cry and a pain-induced cry. A parent can also get to know her baby and what helps him best fall asleep. Some babies sleep really well when they are in a warm and cozy family bed; others babies sleep better in a spacious crib. The American Academy of Pediatrics (AAP) doesn't recommend co-sleeping (parents sleeping with their infants). To reduce the risk of SIDS, the AAP suggests that a new baby should sleep close by in their parent's room, either in a co-sleeper or a crib, which makes sense.

We loved the cozy-nest—a contraption that fits in the parents' bed to ensure safe sleeping practices. It made nursing baby much easier and gave me peace of mind to hear my little one breathing all night. However, if you are on medication or drink alcohol, never co-sleep: it's not safe. Trust your instincts. I know that if I worked forty hours a week, I'd look forward to snuggling in my bed with my babies—after all, they grow up so fast and will be in college before you know it. Bask in the glory of the bonding and attachment.

Babies Don't Need Flashcards or TV—They Need You

Babies need your time and attention, a predictable environment, and consistent loving caregiving. Dr. Bruce Perry from the Child Trauma Academy has done fascinating research around the predictability of children's environments. A child will be fulfilled and emotionally balanced if his parents provide a nurturing and rich social environment on a familiar and sustained basis.

Perry speaks about the attentive parent who gives her baby the necessary "somatosensory bath": hugging, rocking, kissing, singing, bathing, feeding, and gazing into baby's eyes. This somatosensory bath matures over time and gets replaced by other forms of adult interactions. We can see why adults enjoy being hugged; it takes them back to a time when they felt most safe and loved.

Did you know that you (yes you!) are more captivating and entertaining than any other plaything? Babies love to gaze into your eyes, hear your voice, and watch your facial gestures. Sing, babble, massage, and play peek-a-boo with your baby as a bonding experience. Your baby is watching and she's lurking—even when you think she's not paying attention, she really is. Our children are great imitators, so we need to be on our best behavior. Children begin to imitate those they spend the most time with—and this behavior takes roots very early on.

Infants and toddlers learn about their world by first observing and then practicing. If we set good examples, then our children will take notice and begin to follow suit. The same goes for negative examples. If you use foul language and have angry outbursts, then your child will mimic your style when he has the opportunity. Children don't know any better and will take the lead from the most trusted people in their lives—their parents.

If you notice that your baby is nearing ten months old and is not reciprocating your interactions (for example, not cooing back at you or smiling) or avoids eye contact, call your pediatrician immediately. Early intervention is quite effective for children with special needs.

Activities That Foster Bonding and Healthy Communication

- **Babble back and forth with baby.** Babies love to be talked to. Sit face-to-face with baby (a bouncy chair is ideal for this). When baby makes a sound, repeat his sound. This creates confidence and boosts your baby's self-esteem; he knows that Mommy and Daddy not only watch also but listen.

- **Indulge in the moment of sensory play.** Rub your face with the satin of your baby's blanket and say, "Oh, that's soft." Then rub your baby's cheek or leg with the blanket and say, "Do you like that? Is that soft?" Pause and wait for a response. If your baby giggles or pushes her hands out with joy, continue the game.

- **Use movement and singing to engage your baby in physical play.** Babies love to hear their parent's voice. Sing before you put a CD on. Hold your baby and gently bounce to the rhythm of your voice. You can even ask, "Would you like some music?" Then put on a CD.

- **Be a constant talk show.** Babies learn to speak by listening to what you say. Before picking your baby up to change a diaper, first say, "I am going to pick you up—it's diaper time!" Or "It's time to eat; are you hungry?"

- **Start empathy training early.** Babies learn empathy by being cared for and loved. Why not verbalize the cues you see in your baby? You can say, "Oh, I see you're upset. Mama is here; it will be okay." Or if baby is teething, you can say, "It hurts to get new teeth. Mama will help you. It's going to be okay; I'm here."

Guidance and Redirection

To discipline means to guide. After you've baby-proofed your home, you'll find there are things that simply can't be baby-proofed! As your child begins to crawl, redirection and diversion are the most effective tactics for keeping him safe. Save the command "No!" for the big problems—like grabbing your hot coffee or running into danger. If you overuse "No," he'll eventually tune you out. Show him what he can have and redirect.

Using the simple phrase "Not for baby" lets her know that the item or area is not for babies. Show her what *is* okay for babies. Give her a new item of interest or move her to another exciting location. You'll have to do this frequently, but eventually she'll get it.

BLANKETS, STUFFED ANIMALS, AND PACIFIERS

A few years ago I was asked to be CEO of a baby blanket company, but opted to consult instead. I conducted parent focus groups to see if parents knew the true value of having their babies attach to blankets or stuffed animals. Until then I had no idea how many parents take their child's blanket away from her at an early age, thinking it was the "right" time—or how many parents didn't even want their baby to attach to anything. Most parents felt it was keeping their child in the baby stage for too long.

I'll never forget one man who began to cry after our group session—he finally understood the importance and symbolism of his son's blanket. I had explained to the group that a lovey, or comfort object, helps children of all ages develop self-soothing skills. Because very young children have difficulty regulating their emotions, a transitional object is a conduit to emotional well-being. Blankies become a symbol for the parents or caregiver—they provide safety and joy. The child who bonds with a blanket is attaching to a parent substitute. That's why children demand to take their blankie to preschool and on outings.

This father admitted that he took his son's blankie away when the child was four (his son is now eighteen). The dad said that he didn't feel a need for his son to carry around a baby blanket when he was no longer a baby. He told the group he would have never taken that blanket away if he had known just how important it was (that is, a symbol of him).

Babies tend to bond with blankets and stuffed animals between the ages of five and nine months—when they begin to grasp objects and are realizing their separateness from their parents and are moving toward independence. Of course they can bond to objects when they're older, but this is the ideal time.

When you introduce a blanket and stuffed animals to your baby, be sure to have more than one. Wash and rotate them equally so that baby bonds to them all. Both my sons have a couple of miniature blankets, which they call "Mimi's"—God forbid if one ever got lost! My childhood blanket is currently stowed away in my keepsake chest—I even took it to college! It tickles me when my sons ask, "Mommy, where is your Mimi?"

The Pacifier Controversy

What about pacifiers, you ask? If you think your child is going to be taking his pacifier off to college, think again! Most children give up their pacifiers at around three years old. As children grow older, peer pressure becomes more of a factor and may actually be all the incentive a child needs to let go of his treasured pacifier.

A pacifier provides a serene state of calm for infants and young children—and the American Academy of Pediatrics states that pacifier use can actually prevent SIDS; sucking on a pacifier forces the airway to stay open. Pacifier use is now recommended at nap time and bedtime throughout the first year of life. A binky, or pacifier, is also a transitional object that helps relieve stress as children adjust to new situations.

I took my first son's pacifier away when he was nine months old because his nighttime dependence on it was problematic. We were up two to three times every night searching for it, so we opted to banish it. Fortunately he had a very calm temperament and was disgruntled for only two days.

However, my second son is three, and he gave up his pacifier only very recently. He is very high energy and persistent in temperament, and is not easy to console, but once he had his soft blankie and pacifier he immediately calmed down. What parent doesn't need that kind of help every now and then? We slowly weaned him from the pacifier because he speaks much better without it. (We used the fourth method in the list that follows.) When he found his very last pacifier with a hole in it, he tossed it in the trash, then walked away. I expected a meltdown and was ready to call in the rescue team, but he gave up that last faulty pacifier within seconds. I do believe I was more traumatized than he was!

If you choose to decrease pacifier dependency, you can

- Offer it with a satin-trimmed blanket or stuffed animal, so that when he gives up the pacifier, he will still have other comfort objects.
- Limit the use of pacifiers to the bed and car only.
- Work out a deal with your child that the pacifier cannot travel or leave the house.
- Cut one millimeter off the tip of a few—not all—pacifiers in the house. When your child discovers the "broken" pacifier, simply explain that pacifiers eventually break and that her others may break as well. This allows her to get used to the concept of life without the pacifier—which is a hard transition.
- Have a party to give the pacifier away to a new baby. (Good luck with this one!)
- Tie it to balloons and have a launching ceremony. Tell your child that the balloons will take the pacifier to a newborn baby who needs it now.

Thumb Sucking

The baby who sucks her thumb has found a way to soothe herself. How wonderful is that? The advantage of the thumb is that it is always there, whereas a pacifier has to be given by the parent. However, some parents may have feelings of shame and aversion about thumb sucking because they think their child will continue this behavior the rest of his life.

Thumb sucking is quite natural and should only be a concern if your child does it all day. Young children suck their thumbs to calm themselves or to relax, so if you notice that it is happening every minute, you may want to take a close look at what stresses or issues your child may be experiencing. The truth is that healthy

> # Thumbs Up for Thumb Sucking
>
> According to the American Academy of Pediatric Dentistry (AAPD) policy on oral habits, thumb sucking or the sucking on pacifiers is normal in infants and young children.

and secure children will usually stop sucking their thumb by age five, as peer pressure will most likely kick in.

Babies need to find a self-soothing pattern, and sucking their fingers or thumb may just be the most natural path for them. Because I nursed my first son, he had plenty of suckling time. However, as he got older and nursing decreased, he chose to stroke the satin of his blankie to calm down. He was an easy baby to calm, so I was lucky. At night as we watched on the monitor, we'd see him wake, and wait to see if he'd cry for us. Surprisingly, he'd grab his blankie, then fall back to sleep. He never used his thumb, possibly because we gave him a pacifier at five months of age.

My second baby didn't suck his thumb either, and this could have been because I was intent on having him use a pacifier. I introduced it to him a few days after he was born when he showed us he could nurse successfully. I am "propacifier," and as I mentioned, I still let him use it at age three. He's very difficult to console and prefers a pacifier to my husband or me when he is having a meltdown—more power to him. We honor his uniqueness and acknowledge that no two siblings are alike.

No one really can predict just how long a child will continue to suck her thumb. I have an adult client in my practice who grew up in a chaotic home and depended on his thumb to bring him peace and comfort. When I asked what he did to calm himself as an adult, I expected to hear something like, "I read a book, have a beer, or watch TV," but instead he said, "I sometimes suck my thumb." This is a rare case, but I'm sure it's more prevalent than we might assume. And why not? We all have our way of self-soothing, and certainly private thumb sucking is better than more destructive self-medication.

THE IMPORTANCE OF EVENING ROUTINES

The more relaxed your child is, the more likely he'll go to bed easily and fall asleep quickly. Observing a regular wind-down time and consistent nightly rituals is soothing and allows children to feel safe, secure, and sleepy. Without a routine, your child may have difficulties settling down for a good night's sleep. Start the nighttime ritual early in the evening so that you have time to get through all of it before you tuck him in. Begin the routine in the bathroom or in another room and end up in your child's room.

Suggested Nighttime Routines

- Take a bath or wash hands and face.
- Wipe gums or brush teeth.
- Change her diaper and have her get into her PJs.
- Work out the wiggles. Children sometimes get bursts of energy right before they go to sleep, so let them get the nighttime goofies, jump up and down, or have a giggle and tickle session.
- Sing or play a game, but don't get your child overstimulated!
- Read a book out loud. Even children under six months enjoy being read to, and gradually become familiar with words and stories. Mostly they love the sound of your soothing voice.
- Have a goodnight puppet show.
- Say goodnight to things around the house.

- Play soothing music, turn on a white-noise machine, or both.
- End each departure with a tagline: "Mama loves you; see you in the morning" or "Sweet dreams; we all love you."

RESTLESS NIGHTS

New babies are just learning how to adjust to sleeping patterns, so nighttime wakings can have a variety of causes. If your baby isn't sick or doesn't have an ear infection (my sons had many that only woke them in the evenings), most likely she is teething. The teething baby tends to wake up crying with her fingers in her mouth and will drool during the day. Sometimes this is accompanied by a fever. During the tough teething nights, we'd bring our son into our bed and let him suck on a cold washcloth. His teething was once so bad that I let him play with a bowl of ice—which immediately took his mind off the pain. But in the end it was the baby Motrin that worked best.

The other restless nights that may keep baby up are those right before he enters a new stage of development. T. Berry Brazelton coined the term Touchpoints™ to describe how when children show a sudden burst in one area of development, they often "regress," or backslide, in another area. This can be stressful to parents because Touchpoints disorganize children's behavior and routines. However, being aware of this phenomenon helps parents carefully watch and understand their child's behavior and strengths.

I've heard dozens of mothers mention that the day before their baby took his first steps, he was up all night. Both my sons were up crying a lot during the middle of the night the day before they walked.

Some parents have mentioned that their baby had a few fitful nights and days leading up to their child's vocabulary burst of new words. My second son was up for three nights, rolling around, not sleeping well, when lo and behold, the third morning he sprung three new words on us in one day. We were so shocked and excited—aren't babies just the most amazing beings?

So the next time your baby keeps you up all night, there might be something to look forward to in the morning!

TAKING BABY OUT

Sometimes new parents are afraid to take their new bundle of joy out in public. This may have a lot to do with the mother's perception of how she'll be viewed in public with a screaming child.

If a mother becomes tuned in to her baby, then she learns when *not* to take baby out, such as during nap hours or feeding times. However, the nursing mother has the lovely advantage of being able to take baby everywhere and nurse whenever need be. The nursing mother's challenge is to find a private and soothing place to feed her baby. If she knows when baby usually feeds, she should try not to do her grocery shopping during that time.

The key is to think ahead. If you know that baby is easier in the morning, then that would be the best time to go out and run an errand. If all baby needs is Mommy's smile or a pacifier, then the venture may be worth the trip! If you know that baby takes her marathon nap midday in her car seat carrier, then that would be a great time to bring her to have lunch with your friends.

Being Prepared

You probably know by now that it is okay to go out with baby once your pediatrician gives you permission. If the baby is a newborn (yes, newborns are allowed to go out!), then you will usually want someone along to help out.

Moms usually feel more comfortable going out with baby after the first two to three months of life, which I call the adjustment phase. Be sure to dress baby appropriately for the weather. This is a great time to show off your sweet baby outfits, cute blankies, cool carrier-pouch-sling, or tricked-out stroller.

Give baby lots of practice going out by taking regular walks in the stroller, backpack, or sling. And don't forget the car! Baby also needs to get used to traveling in the car in her car seat. If your baby is consistently out and about, then she will be less likely to see "going out" as a stressful experience.

I dined out with my children as babies on a regular basis, and till this day, they view restaurants as a normal place to eat. Choose baby- and child-friendly destinations. I like to shop at Nordstrom because when my son got fussy, I'd head to the nursing area in its restroom. Once he was done feeding, I could shop a little more. I'd even have my friends meet me there for coffee! All of this gave me the confidence to be a go-out type of mommy.

I'd run errands during my son's long sleeping jags. He'd fall asleep in his portable infant seat carrier, and I'd go to the grocery store, pharmacy, or post office. Sometimes I'd even sneak in a pedicure!

Most people love babies, so take your baby on outings as much as you can. You'll find during the most stressful situations that many strangers have compassion—unless you're on an airplane. That can be a whole different story!

Your Attitude Is an Important Factor

If Mom and Dad hold the view that taking a newborn out is normal, then baby will share that energy. Just because a baby cries in public doesn't mean she doesn't like being out. We all know that our babies cry a lot when we're home! Take the leap and have the confidence to go out and show the world how great it is to be a new parent. Here are some more tips:

- Bring someone to help.
- Invest in a portable infant car seat carrier that attaches to a stroller frame.

- Regularly offer an attachment object beginning when your baby is three months old (or when baby begins to reach out with her hand). Bring her attachment object (pacifier, blanket, or stuffed animal) with you for comfort.

- Scope out a place to nurse when you arrive at your destination.

- Be prepared to make a bottle if you're not nursing.

- If baby is eating, bring snacks and full sippy cups.

- Have a full diaper bag—wipes, diapers, and cream.

- Bring two extra pairs of clothes. (Babies spit up and poop in rapid-fire succession!)

- Learn nursery rhymes or baby songs: baby loves to hear you sing.

- Bring a rattle or toy with a bell for you to shake and entertain her with.

- If baby fusses, keep your energy calm, even if you feel embarrassed. Take the experience in stride and let baby know you understand how she feels and that you're there for her.

- Be ready at any time to leave your destination and feel good about it. It's time for Mommy to accommodate baby, not the other way around.

Your trip out with baby will be an enjoyable one as long as you know there's a place to nurse, a place to change a diaper, and a place for baby to sleep.

Traveling and Vacationing with Baby—Do It While You Can

At some point or another, you may want to travel or take a vacation with baby. This is the best age to travel because baby is not walking or talking and basically sleeps anywhere, so take advantage and plan a trip away from home. Trust me—it was a lot easier to travel when I could cuddle baby and carry him in a front-pack carrier than it is now, when he is walking and exerting his new-found independence!

Have a good attitude and tell yourself that it's okay to travel and that baby will actually enjoy the trip. This good positive energy is contagious.

Here are some things to keep in mind:

- Look for a pediatrician in the area you're traveling to, and have his or her number handy in case baby gets sick. Ask the people you're visiting for recommendations, or have your health care provider give you a list of doctors in the area. You can also do an Internet search and then call the office to see if the doctor will accept a new patient and your insurance.
- Be sure to bring the necessary baby accoutrements:
  - Pack-n-play portable crib
  - Nursing gear
  - Baby front pack or sling carrier
  - Extra blankets
  - Extra bottles
  - Extra clothes
  - Extra diapers
  - Snacks
  - Formula
  - Toys and teethers
- Entertain baby:
  - Bring out toys, rattles, bells, books, and so on—one by one. You want to keep baby contented as long as possible, so don't use up all your tricks too early.
  - Sing to baby or have your partner sing.

If you're flying:

- Nurse baby during takeoff and landing or have pacifier or bottle ready to help with releasing inner-ear pressure.
- If baby fusses, walk him around and talk to other people. Babies love new faces.

It's always best to travel with someone who'll help. It's easier to maintain a good attitude if you have support. Anyway, isn't the whole idea of traveling that you and your family can have nice time away from home?

DEALING WITH SEPARATION ANXIETY

Babies can show signs of separation anxiety as early as six months, but the toughest time for most babies is between thirteen to twenty months. That's when your baby is becoming a toddler and realizing that she is a completely separate being from you. Even nighttime fussing can be an expression of separation anxiety—sleep is a scary separation for little ones. Toddlers understand about people leaving before they learn about people returning. They can tell from your actions that you're about to leave. Anxiety begins to build even before you have a foot out the door. And anxiety can be contagious. The more anxious you are about leaving or about others caring for your baby, the more anxious your baby will be.

Separation anxiety shows up in many forms. Your child may cry when you leave the room or refuse to be put down if she knows you'll be leaving. Some children will follow their parents into every room all day long. One of the hardest scenarios for parents to deal with is dropping their clingy and crying toddler off at day care. It can tug at your heartstrings and make you doubt yourself and your decisions.

The good news is that separation anxiety will pass and that there are ways to make it more manageable.

Ways to Help You and Your Child Adjust to Times of Separation

- **Offer a transitional object.** Encourage your child to attach to a transitional object, such as a blanket or stuffed toy that he can hold on to. Introducing such an object early in infancy encourages attachment to soothing things. Babies love satin. Rubbing the satin takes them back to the safety and security of the womb.
- **Practice taking breaks away.** If you know you're going to be away for a longer than normal period, help your child work up to that separation by taking a series of short breaks, such as by going next door for a minute or running a brief errand. Practice separations; tell your baby that you'll be going to another room and you'll be back soon.
- **Have your sitter come early.** If someone is coming to watch your child, have him or her come early so that all of you can spend some time together before you leave.
- **Leave on a happy note.** You want your baby to associate happy thoughts with your coming and going. Don't sneak away. Even though this makes it easier for you, it isn't easier on your toddler. Let him see you leave, even if he has tears. If you continue to sneak off, he'll become even more worried that you might disappear at any random time. Say your bye-byes and then help him become involved in a fun activity that will occupy him as you leave.
- **Ditch the guilt.** Finally, don't feel guilty about your child's teary emotions. Just know that this is a stage and that you'll both get through it! Don't minimize her experience by getting resentful or angry if she goes into a tirade when you leave. It's quite normal to feel at peace with your child's neediness at one moment and then to feel agitated and overwhelmed the next. Try to find ways to balance your need for her

independence with her needs to expand her world and feel safe.

BEGINNING TO SOCIALIZE

Babies are very social beings. It's never too early to begin socializing your baby with other babies similar in age. Babies are fascinated by each other and will often reach out and try to touch one another, which is an indicator that they do enjoy and benefit from early socialization.

Parents need to get out, too, to build their social networks and support systems. I started a neighborhood playgroup, which proved to be invaluable. Many of my neighbors serve as surrogate aunties and uncles who come in handy when I need babysitting.

Baby and Me or gym classes are a good place to start. Attending a playgroup or high-quality child-care program is also a wonderful way for your child to interact with other children and a great way to learn about the world in which they live.

Parents need contact or hangout time with other parents who have similar-aged children. It's no fun to parent in a vacuum, so make a point of striking up new relationships with moms who have kidlings similar in age to yours. Making friends can be easy. You can start a conversation with another parent in the market, at the park, or in your child's gym class. If you're a mom and your husband clearly isn't going to gab the gab or dish the mommy-talk, you'll benefit from having a circle of cool and fun mommy friends.

Starting a Playgroup

Have dreams of running an organized and hot-to-trot playgroup? Child rearing today can be more challenging because parents are opting to have children later in life and have less energy and experience and fewer resources. Families take months off from work to care for their new baby, but usually one parent chooses to go back to work full-time while the other stays home. Can one person possibly meet all the physical, social, emotional, intellectual, linguistic, spiritual, and cultural needs of her growing children? Not easily. Involvement in a regular playgroup just may be the answer.

The most successful playgroups are lead by organized, friendly, diplomatic individuals. Here's how to get started:

- Create a fun name for your group.
- Put together a newsletter, flyer, Web site, or some combination of these.
- Pick a location, such as the local park or your backyard.
- Solicit families you see strolling.
- Create an online e-mail roster.
- Encourage families to host groups at their home.
- Vote for a new group president each year.
- Have fun and enjoy getting to know neighbors and their children.

I started my playgroup when my first boy was a year old, and it grew into a local community group of more than sixty families. After five years, the group was still going strong, and I'm so thankful we have other families to lean on in times of need. Starting your own playgroup may feel overwhelming at first, but the benefits are well worth it.

PREVENTING BURNOUT BY ACCEPTING HELP

Who said raising kids and managing a family were easy or should be a solo gig? If you're employed, then you're on triple-work duty. Even if you take time off to raise kids, accept all the help you can get. If someone offers to bring food, do laundry, watch your kids, or pick up groceries, your response should always be "Yes, thank you." You won't be putting the person out. In fact, people like to help because it feels good. (And during the times when you don't need help, spread the goodness around by lending a hand to others in your playgroup.)

It's not easy asking for help. You may think that just because you wanted to be a parent, you have to rise to the occasion *all the time*. This is a misconception that can take you straight down the road to burnout. You can ask for a little aid. You will find that by asking your friends or family for a hand, life is a lot more manageable. Sometimes people don't know how to help, and they'll appreciate it and be more likely to assist if you're clear and concise with your needs.

If you don't have a playgroup, family, or friends nearby or willing to help, there's no harm in hiring someone. Whether you're employed or you stay at home with the kids, there's great peace of mind in knowing that steady help is available, and what better way to guarantee that than by paying someone?

TEACHING THE WORD "HELP" AS ONE OF YOUR BABY'S FIRST WORDS

Before they learn to speak words, babies and toddlers have to rely on crying as their primary means of communication. Babies begin to understand language as early as nine months of age, so you can expect that some of your baby's first words will be spoken shortly after her first birthday or even later if your child is a boy. Some parents use sign language to communicate with their preverbal baby. I taught both my babies how to say the word "Help"—and boy did it dramatically decrease all the screaming and frustration.

When your child needs your help, walk over to her and acknowledge her feelings: "You're frustrated. Need help?" Then continue to use only one-word statements when you hear her cry: "Help. Mama helps."

After a few days of this, her cries may cease and be replaced with her saying, "Help, help."

Life will be a lot less stressful when the screaming stops. Once you know she's not hurt, you can tend to her needs because she'll have learned the basic word "Help."

WHEN MOMS GO TO WORK

Not all moms are able to stay at home, and many are not cut out for it. Many women, both married and single, have to work out of financial necessity. Others choose to work to keep their sanity, to remain competitive in their field, or for the rewards that come from their accomplishments. It is not up to any of us to judge what another mother needs or does. What's most important is to enjoy your time with your children and to be sure you have sufficient time to create a meaningful and significant bond. A happy and confident mom, whether she works in or out of the home (or both) breeds happy and secure children.

Within three months of both my boys' being born, I went back to consulting. I've never really stopped working, and I've been lucky to be able to work at home and also go out to see clients. Staying home all day became too monotonous for me, and I yearned to be around adults to exercise my intellect. I opted to have my babies in a high-quality child-care center two days per week for three hours.

Were you told that by staying home, you were offering your child the best life experience possible? Research shows that high-quality child development centers tend to meet the myriad of needs that the working parent simply can't provide on a daily basis. Good centers offer opportunities for children to socialize, play, experiment, and interact with others their age in an environment that's designed to meet their developmental needs.

Look for licensed facilities that have low child-teacher ratios and are accredited by the National Association of Education of

Young Children (NAEYC). Any licensed early childhood center will allow you to drop in without prior notice.

STAYING CONNECTED

At what point do we parents need to disconnect from our kids to promote resiliency and self-responsibility? Never. We just need to give them space to grow, both emotionally and socially.

For each critical stage of development, a child needs something completely different from his parents. A three-year-old clearly needs heightened supervision, whereas a nine-year-old may need time alone to complete his new science project without adult interference. A five-year-old may still want Mom to hold his hand on the way to kindergarten, whereas a twelve-year-old needs more physical and emotional space from Mom as he enters preadolescence.

However, none of the stages of a child's life warrants disconnection. Both the child and her parents benefit from knowing all that goes on in the child's world. This does not mean that we are entitled to read our child's journal, but we do need to take interest and be actively involved in all that she does—no matter what her age.

No child will flourish or benefit from isolation, no matter how much he may ask for it when he becomes a teenager.

THE GO-TO MOM'S QUICK AND NIFTY TIPS

When in Doubt, Call a Parent

Have you ever had a problem, then picked up the phone and your friend solved the issue immediately? That always happens for me.

Sometimes we are too close to the problem and need a fresh perspective from someone who's been there, done that. What better way to get that than by asking a mom or dad?

Make Baby Snacks Accessible

Once baby learns how to crawl, try putting a few snacks in BPA-free clear Lucite containers on a low shelf. He can crawl to his snack and choose what he'd like to eat. He'll enjoy the opportunity to make his own snack choice.

Keep Cats out of the Crib

Cats are fearful of balloons, so before you bring baby home or when baby's not in her crib or bassinet, put a few balloons in there. Kitty will stay out for sure. When you remove the balloons, check to see that no balloons have popped—and be sure that no pieces are left in the crib.

Make the Changing Table Entertaining

As your baby gets older, she may start to resist her diaper change. Keep a basket of "attention keepers" close at hand and say, "Look at this!" then give her an interesting item. This may stop her from trying to roll off the changing table.

Keep the Pacifier Handy

Tired of dropping the pacifier on the dirty floor while holding your bundle of joy? Try threading the hole of the pacifier onto the end of a burp cloth or bib. Toss the burp cloth over your shoulder, or have baby wear the bib. Of course this will only work with pacifiers that have a hole, such as Nuk.

The Terrific Twos and Terrible Threes

Moving from New and Exciting to Sweat and Tears

> Good parenting begins in your heart, and then
> continues on a moment-to-moment basis by
> engaging your children when feelings run high,
> when they are sad, angry, or scared. The heart of
> parenting is being there in a particular way when it
> really counts.
>
> —John Gottman

So you've begun to be an emotion coach as your child learns to walk, talk, and enter into the terrible twos—or as we now call them, the terrific twos! You may find that once your child becomes two and then three, you'll be tested the most so far. During this stage, you have the most work and also a great deal of responsibility, because you'll be influencing and shaping your child's emotion vocabulary to a great degree.

What was once a happy-go-lucky baby is now a whirlwind of energy! Not only will your amazingly brilliant child be exploring the world—she'll be rapidly learning new words, phrases, and an attitude to go with them! As you did with the young toddler, however, you can still use guidance and redirection, and once your child begins to speak, you should be moving toward using the actual emotion coaching steps (discussed in Chapter Two). You can begin to wean your child off the redirection and distraction when he's in danger or not cooperating.

SETTING LIMITS

It's important for parents to be sensitive to the difference between redirection for control and redirection for growth and happy development. If you redirect a verbal child, it may come off as minimizing or denying her desires. Because your child is now able to speak, you must honor her advances and become more sophisticated with your discipline tactics. In this chapter, I've outlined many common parenting tactics that clearly don't work with children—and I offer more effective approaches that you can use to stay connected with your children while still setting firm limits that bring about cooperation.

Emotion coaching is not effective alone—as parents we must set limits on what is acceptable and not acceptable throughout our child's life. The two most important things you can do is provide unconditional love and set clear, concise rules. Our children rely on us to establish age-appropriate expectations. Parents who don't reinforce or set limits have children who may have a difficult time understanding the function and importance of boundaries. In society there are clearly things that one can and cannot do, and for most people, this concept is learned within the home. Children will always push their limits—it's a natural part of the human condition—but it's your job as a parent to guide, shape, and take a proactive role in helping them develop healthy social skills.

Setting limits or coming up with family rules doesn't involve frightening or threatening your child. You do let him know what is "okay" and "not okay." Because children are continually learning and developing a sense of morality, you must offer a brief explanation of why they can or can't do something. Parents who use reason and logic have children who cooperate more often than parents who use the "Because I said so" philosophy.

Just because you have family rules set in stone won't guarantee that your children will always comply or be happy with them. In fact, well-adjusted kids act out more at home, where they feel safe and secure, than any other place. Your kids will push your buttons, and all you can do is be prepared! Be loving and firm, act in accordance with your own rules, and remember that all feelings are okay—there are no right or wrong feelings. All emotions are a part of the human condition. Other critical needs for humans are to feel industrious, competent, and powerful.

CHILDREN NEED TO FEEL POWERFUL

Children need to feel powerful and independent in order to feel fully competent. The child who feels little power throughout her day may create negative opportunities to feel powerful—which may take the form of oppositional behavior or intentional power struggles with others. Children will make good choices when they feel we respect them, as demonstrated by our continuous efforts to give them appropriate control over their lives.

If you want your children to have freedom and to feel confident with their decisions, then you need to set up their environment for success—which often means helping them feel in control. You don't want to constantly deny their personal choices either, so don't take them into a toy or candy store if you know they won't be able to control themselves and you'll have to keep saying no. Provide a natural setting and monitor their environment so that health and social responsibility are the norm—this includes protecting your child from exposure to weapons, drugs, inappropriate or violent media, and the like.

Preschoolers spend a lot time in the egocentric stage—which in plain talk means, "All About Me." So no matter how hard you try to avoid that meltdown or tantrum, as a parent you are bound to witness many. When you feel the tug-of-war begin with your child, drop the rope. There can be no struggle unless two people are pulling—which is always against each other. As clichéd it sounds, "Choose your battles."

WHY SPANKING DOESN'T WORK

Many parents are coming to grips with the fact that spanking their children doesn't work. Spankings teach only a short-term lesson, and come with a host of potential undesirable outcomes in adulthood.

The Best Development Occurs in Nurturing and Violence-Free Environments

Remember when you were little and everything was so exciting to you? You may have felt that the world was a fun place to be—life without judgment, responsibilities, or a job to tend to—you were free to do whatever was enjoyable and interesting. That time is when you probably learned the most.

As I discussed in Chapter Three, early childhood is a very sensitive and critical time for brain development. Stress caused by fear of spanking can have a negative effect on the development and function of a child's brain. It is during this period of great plasticity and vulnerability that many children are subjected to physical punishment.

According to researcher Dr. Martin Teicher of McLean Hospital in Massachusetts, "We know that an animal exposed to stress and neglect in early life develops a brain that is wired to experience fear, anxiety and stress. We think the same is true of people."

I don't know any parent who would intentionally put his or her child at risk for abnormal brain development; however, that is often what spankers do.

Spanking Impairs the Ability to Learn and to Perform in School

Research has shown that spanking a child lowers his IQ. When a child is in a calm and nonthreatened state, the brain is primed to learn. However, if spanking a child makes him feel angry or scared, he becomes hypervigilant, and learning comes to a screeching halt. Children who are taught to fear regular spankings tend to live in a semiagitated state that is not conducive to optimal learning.

We see that children who exhibit the most serious behavior problems at school often have a troubled home life. This sets them up for academic failure, dropping out, teen pregnancy, and drug use. In their attempt to protect themselves from a comfortless and aggressive parent, these children naturally affiliate with others who have similar problems. They may join a gang to find a new family that can fill the void created by a failed home life.

Advice from a Professor of Psychiatry

Researchers have also found that children who are spanked show higher rates of aggression and delinquency in childhood than those who were not spanked. As adults, they are more prone to depression, feelings of alienation, use of violence toward a spouse, and lower economic and professional achievement. None of this is what we want for our children.
—Alvin Poussaint, MD, Professor of Psychiatry, Harvard Medical School, "Spanking Strikes Out," from FamilyEducation.com, September 27, 1999

Spanking Teaches Children That It Is Okay to Use Violence

Children see their parents as role models. You can't tell your child to stop hitting her siblings if you are hitting her as a method of discipline. This only confuses your child. If your child does what he's told because of a spanking, the lesson you've taught is, "Violence works." And you can bet that he'll learn from your actions and, as a result, use force to win in other situations. When your child grows up, do you want him to discuss problems with his spouse or use force to settle conflict?

Advice from a Religious Leader

I have never accepted the principle of "spare the rod and spoil the child." . . . I am persuaded that violent fathers produce violent sons. . . . Children don't need beating. They need love and encouragement. They need fathers to whom they can look with respect rather than fear. Above all, they need example.

— Gordon B. Hinckley, president, the Church of Jesus Christ of Latter-day Saints, General Conference, October 1994

We all know the red flags and the possible roots of violent criminal behavior: poverty, discrimination, family breakdown, drugs, gangs, and easy access to deadly weapons. Jordan Riak, the founder of Parents and Teachers Against Violence in Education, Inc., states, "Every item listed above contributes to violence and crime, but what about spanking?"

Researchers Sheldon and Eleanor Glueck conducted a landmark study of delinquent and nondelinquent boys. They discovered how certain early childhood influences cause children to develop antisocial, violent behaviors. In their findings, signs of delinquency appeared in children as young as three—long before children come into contact with influences outside the home. The Gluecks showed that parents who fail to manage their children calmly, gently, and patiently, but instead rely on physical punishment, tend to produce aggressive, assaultive children. The more severe and the earlier the mistreatment, the worse the outcome. They also found that the lowest incidence of antisocial behavior is associated with children who are reared from infancy in attentive, supportive, nonviolent families.

If you want to do everything within your power to prevent your child from continuing the harmful legacy of spanking when he's a parent, guide gently, set appropriate limits, and emotion coach as much as you possibly can. Stay away from the four common roadblocks (outlined in Chapter One) that make parenting challenging and ineffective, and don't ever spank.

Hitting Can Lead to Injuries

Those who support spanking say it's okay if it's deliberate and methodical. "Never spank in anger," they say. This message implies that hurting a child is acceptable as long it's done calmly. But research shows that over time a parent who spanks tends to hit harder each time. When spankings lose the desired effect, parents tend toward using too much force, putting children at risk for injury.

Many parents defend their right to spank because it provides them with an outlet for frustration and anger with their child—not because it's an effective way to improve their child's behavior. There is never a right time or safe way to hit a child, because acts of violence, by their very nature, tend to escalate as time goes on.

Hitting Children Destroys Their Self-Esteem

Do you remember how you felt after you were hit? You probably felt anger, sadness, and confusion, and you may have even felt unloved. Although parents don't intend for their child to feel these things, most often they do.

Many people say, "I was spanked and turned out just fine" or "I deserved to be hit because I was a bad kid." People make these statements and become defensive because it's painful to admit that their parents, the ones who should have protected them, did something terribly wrong. We all see our parents as the most important people in our lives, and if we admit that they've done us wrong or are pathological, it might mean that we too are faulty or damaged goods. It's a defense that protects us from feeling abandoned—so we defend our parents no matter what wrong they've done. It's hard to admit that we do this, but it's true.

Consider This

Why is it that hitting an animal is called cruelty, hitting an adult is called battery, and hitting a child is called discipline?

—Anonymous

As children become adults, they adopt some of their parents' positive qualities. If you were spanked and feel you turned out to be a good person, it's not because of the spankings. Many of us who were spanked on occasion are great, successful people—but it's *despite* the spankings, not because of them.

What to Do Instead of Spanking

There are better ways of teaching children how to be cooperative. Fear and aggression are not effective. The true meaning of the word *discipline* is "to guide." Guidance means teaching. When we punish children, we leave out the guidance.

Children learn good behavior by imitating good behavior. Children learn morals, values, and compassion from their parents. To prepare your child to enter into a healthy adult life with valuable skills, practice teaching her the value of self-motivation, and how to negotiate, compromise, and resolve conflicts successfully and nonaggressively.

Here are a variety of nonaggressive alternatives that you can use to guide your children.

- Get in touch with your own "hot buttons" and be sure not to take your anger and problems over some unresolved conflicts of your own out on your child.
- Take a grown-up "cool-off" time when you find yourself too angry to deal with your child.
- Begin providing guidance and setting limits as early as infancy.
- Keep communicating your thoughts and feelings with your baby and young child.
- Discuss your feelings about what you see.
- Acknowledge and validate your child's feelings while setting limits.
- Offer alternatives.
- Redirect your child's attention.
- Be consistent and follow through (do what you say you're going to do).
- Offer encouragement when your child follows through.
- Offer a "thinking time" or "cool-down time." If your child is over three years old, have her sit with you and think about her actions and ask her what she can do differently next time. (I discuss this approach in the next section.)
- Offer solutions or brainstorm ideas with your child—sometimes she may not know what to do and needs your guidance.

WHY TIME-OUTS DON'T WORK

Can you believe there are parents who post their child's time-out videos on YouTube? Many of these children are under two years of age—still in diapers. Is this an avenue for parents to display how funny it is to see a young child being disciplined, as if it were entertainment? It is virtually impossible for a child two years of age or younger to understand what a time-out is, let alone understand why their parents have such high expectations for them when they have such little life experience.

Both the misuse of time-outs—having them serve as punishment rather than guidance—and the lack of respect that underlies parents' willingness to distribute videos of a child's embarrassing moments, make this type of treatment abusive. It's humiliating enough for a child to be disciplined in private, but then to post it on the Internet? What purpose does this serve? As Alfie Kohn states in his book *Unconditional Parenting*, "Many parents are cracking down on their young children just for being kids, which is heartbreaking to watch." Parents who understand children's developmental limitations tend to respond to their children in a reasonable, calm, and patient manner.

Research shows that creating a stronger bond between parent and child involves empathy. Empathy is the foundation for effective parenting—in fact, the more empathy a parent has for his young child, the stronger the relationship and thus the less acting out. Toddlers have limited emotion regulation and need a caring adult to empathize with them, soothe them, and guide them. Children who are put into repeated time-outs may develop poor emotion control because they are left alone without support and validation during the upheaval. These children are at risk for then being labeled as difficult or, possibly, hyperactive. In a worst-case scenario, these children may react by internalizing the emotional pain (swallowing down or giving up their emotions altogether) in order to cope, which can eventually turn into early childhood depression.

Young Children Don't Understand the Concept of a Time-Out

Parents who give time-outs to very young children usually do so because they lack of knowledge of child development and have unrealistic expectations. When young children are upset, they unravel and spin out of control—stress hormones are released, and the children's ability to take control of their emotions is almost nil. These are the times when they need their parents most. The misuse of a time-out is not only punishing but also alienating, and may spark a long-term physiological response.

If the children in the videos I've seen on YouTube had parents who were more empathic to their needs or who were emotion coaches, there would be less stress and emotional breakdown for them. Parents who empathize with their children understand that a fifteen-month-old simply can't know the true ramifications of spilling his Fruit Loops and stepping on them. He's just playing, and they make a great sound under his feet.

I viewed a two-year-old toddler being made to stand in the corner. Her mom repeatedly asked, "Will you be good?" and the toddler would whimper and shake her head no. This child was shaking her head because all she felt at the moment was "No, I don't like what is happening to me." However, the mother kept insisting that her daughter say, "Yes, Mommy, I'll be good."

This mother didn't understand that toddlers who are under emotional stress (which time-outs can cause) have a hard time understanding language or parental requests. She never clarified what "good" meant, so even if the toddler agreed, she wouldn't have known what she was agreeing to. It's all too likely that she'll end up in the corner again, without even knowing why.

Another video showed a little boy who was about twenty months old—just an innocent child sitting in the corner crying as his father videotaped him. We all know that getting a child to sit at this age is very difficult. I could see that this little boy was sitting not because he was learning a lesson but because he was following directions out of fear of his intimidator—the man with the camera, whom he calls Daddy.

There was also a baby about twelve months old, and his parents had turned his high chair into the corner for a time-out because he was making bubbles into his cereal and spitting it out. His parents laughed at him and said, "I bet you'll never do that again."

These children were being disciplined in a way that parents don't realize will never work . . . and at what cost? Just because the toddlers stopped their poor behavior for the moment doesn't mean they understand what a time-out is. These children stopped their behavior temporarily because they were afraid of their parent's rejection and withdrawal of love, not because they were going to change their behavior forever. Far from it. Research shows that negative motivation doesn't work.

Use a Cool-Down or Thinking Time Instead

A toddler's developing brain cannot process and integrate the complex message of a time-out. I am personally opposed to using the traditional time-out method with children of any age. Sending a child to the corner or to her room will never produce successful results. Children need to know what they can do differently the next time so that they don't repeat the same mistake—and this is best taught through guidance and setting limits, which is the basis of a cool-down time.

For most kids over two, I support the thinking-time method instead of old-school time-outs. The thinking-time method is gentle and nonpunitive; it's designed to keep the parent by the child's side while the parent helps the child learn to calm himself down, think about what he did, and come up with a better solution.

Thinking time, or any variety of time-out for that matter, should not be used with most children under two years of age because, as I said earlier, it simply won't work. Little children don't know what to do unless they're shown. It's a parent's job to guide and teach her child about the world until he is old enough to fly solo. Would you expect an adult to know how to drive a car if he's never been in one before?

Connection is the key ingredient in helping guide our children. Punishment disconnects us from our children and impairs the goal of helping them become self-sufficient. Mary Sheedy Kurcinka, the author of *Kids, Parents, and Power Struggles*, believes that when a parent takes time to listen and respond instead of resorting to alienation or withdrawal of love, the child learns to view the bond as rewarding. Children need their parents to act as role models in building a healthy relationship. When you take time to connect and help your child choose appropriate actions through guidance, then there's no need for emotionally draining time-outs.

The following are steps for using a cool-down or thinking time successfully. Remember: if your child is younger than two years old, use distraction or redirection. *Never* use a thinking time; she's simply too young to understand this concept.

Steps to Successful Use of a Cool-Down or Thinking Time

1. Get down at your child's level. Be sure to have good eye contact; give a warning and ask if what she is doing is "okay" or "not okay."

2. If your child doesn't calm down or stop the unacceptable behavior, then lead him to a "quiet area" or "thinking area." Sit with him and offer assistance and love. Remember, this is *not* a punishment.

3. Time is not important—having your child calm down is. Disregard the "one minute times your child's age" stance that most use as a guide. Don't give a five-year-old "five minutes to think"; sometimes the older child needs only a minute or two

to come up with a better solution. A younger child may need to cuddle or sit with you for ten minutes until she's calm. Empathize, validate, and reflect what you see. An understood child is less likely to be fraught.

4. Once your child is calm, ask him to tell you "what's wrong" or "what's going on." Restate the problem again more clearly if he has difficulty.

5. Ask your child, "What will you do differently next time?" Name the expected behavior if she doesn't know.

6. Thank your child for helping come up with a solution.

7. Set the expectation for the future by wrapping up with, "If you don't listen next time, what will happen?" Inform your child that you will take actions to help and that you will not tolerate unacceptable behavior.

Story of a Successful Cool-Down Time

During a play date, five-year-old Jillian hit three-and-a-half-year-old Lizzy with a Barbie. Jillian's mother walked over to intervene because Lizzy can't formulate her words quickly enough to stop the aggressive exchange.

> *Mom:* Jillian, stop now. (*Mom gently takes the Barbie.*) I see you're angry, but we never hit; we use our words. What are you mad about?
>
> *Jillian:* She took the doll—I want it! (*Jillian continues to push Lizzy.*)
>
> *Mom:* We don't hit. Let's go to cool down in the other room. Lizzy, are you okay? I'm sorry this happened; we'll be back. (*Lizzy's mom consoles Lizzy.*)
>
> *Mom:* (*Now in another room with Jillian*) Jillian, what's going on? You looked really mad. You really wanted that doll.
>
> *Jillian:* I wanted the doll. I love that Barbie.

Mom: That doll is your favorite, I know. Is it okay to hit or push to get your way?

Jillian: No.

Mom: What can you do next time you need some help or get mad? Will you hit or push Lizzy?

Jillian: No. But she can't have my favorite Barbie!

Mom: Tell me what you will do next time you're mad.

Jillian: Not hit.

Mom: What else?

Jillian: Come and get you.

Mom: What about using your words? That helps too.

Jillian: Yes, I will say, "That's my doll!"

Mom: Maybe you can say, "I'm using it now, but when I'm done, you can play with it."

Jillian: Okay, Mama.

Mom: Remember when you're mad to use your words or get a grown-up; never hit. If you hit Lizzy again, what will happen?

Jillian: She'll be sad.

Mom: Yes, she'll be sad, and you will not be able to play with Lizzy. Do you understand? Tell me what you'll do if you get mad again.

Jillian: Use my words and get a grown-up.

Mom: Yes, I trust you will. I love you. Let's go see Lizzy.

As we see here, Jillian's mom chooses the thinking-time method—where time is not an issue. What's important is that Jillian understands that there are other ways to get what she wants and that violence will not be tolerated. But did Jillian need to feel bad or punished to learn that valuable lesson? No. And the bond between Jillian and her mother was not negatively impacted. Jillian's mom removed her because she was physically out of control, but never left her alone. Jillian's mom set limits, while still being loving and understanding. Before she let Jillian go back to play with Lizzy, her mother made sure that Jillian knew the rules and had a tool box filled with solutions to be cooperative.

WHY REWARDS DON'T WORK

Some modern parents have become quite sophisticated in the ways they manipulate their children's behavior. Giving rewards is one popular current method that is simplistic and requires very little interaction or guidance on the parents' part. It's the easy way out. It takes time and effort to figure out why a child may not want to go to school or what fear he may have, but if we promise a milkshake after school, maybe he'll go without a fight.

Some believe that if they attach a positive reward to a desired behavior, their child will keep on cooperating—or that if their child doesn't want to do something, the reward will be an incentive. The problem is, if we keep on giving, they'll keep on expecting . . . and that's not how child development or even our human society works. A child is more likely to work harder for love, attention, connection, and acknowledgment than for a toy. Parents should depend on the strength of the relationship with their child instead of offering up a reward.

Studies have shown that children who expected rewards didn't perform all that well, and actually performed poorly, compared to kids who did not expect a reward. And to top it off, children who are given rewards tend to do the least amount required. Most parents want their kids to try hard at anything they do and to find real fulfillment from within. Clearly, rewards fail to offer this kind of incentive or satisfaction.

How Rewards Can Backfire

Ever wonder why after a few weeks of using a sticker chart, it stops working? Children sense that you're trying to make them do something, and they feel the external push. Children only want to accomplish things successfully when they feel motivated from within.

Here are some of the basic problems that can result from the reward system.

1. Children will do things for the reward or praise and not for themselves. This can stop children from being self-motivated and can make them overly dependent on others. When children get used to receiving rewards for behaving, they become pleasers and seekers of outside validation. External rewards can be addictive as well: children can become attention mongers, and thus lose passion for the things they truly love. Children will eventually feel like failures if they can't get others to make them feel important.

2. Praising a child's potential has a negative impact on their self-worth. Saying things like "I just know you can do it" or "Come on—you can do better!" sounds encouraging but is not—those statements are loaded with expectations that the child must excel. The child only trucks on to keep you happy with her progress. Praising children's potential can make them feel disappointed with who they are. The underlying message is "You're not good enough yet."

3. Rewarding children for being compliant is manipulative. Research shows that parents who use rewards also use punishment. Children don't like to feel controlled and can see praise as condescending. Praise reminds the child that she is being evaluated and judged. Though "Good girl!" may seem like a positive thing to say, it's still a judgment, which makes a child feel accepted only for what she *does* and not for who she *is*. It's better to say, "Wow, you ate the entire dinner—you love green beans!" than to say, "Good girl—you ate all your dinner."

4. Children can detect manipulation from a mile away. That's why they might scowl or turn away after you've said something nice. I would say to my son, "You're so good at math." He'd

reply, "No I'm not! It's hard—will you stop saying that?!" Acknowledgment gets a better response from kids: "I see you did your math quickly. Is it easy for you?" They might reply, "This math sheet is easy—I do it in class all the time—but fractions are hard."

5. Rewards are punishing because they're only offered when the child obeys and are held back if she doesn't comply. Children tend to feel inadequate if the praise or reward doesn't come— they'll always associate being cooperative with a "What will you give me in return?" attitude.

6. When children are bribed with rewards just for being coopera- tive, they become experts in performing the "dog and pony" show. They know what to do to get our approval or the treat. It's easy to be superficially compliant because it doesn't require much effort. If our relationship is reduced to one of mutual manipulation rather than authentic connection, it sets the stage for manipulative and dishonest relationships later in life. Do we want our children to grow up trying hard in order to please? Or do we want them to grow up trying hard because it feels good to them?

7. Children sense it when you impose your own desires on them. Your child can detect when you have praised him because he made you feel good about yourself. This robs him of feeling good about himself. Praise can hamper our children's desires and personal achievement. Children can refuse to produce what they're naturally good at, because they are turned off by their overzealous parents.

If you decide not to use rewards or praise, it doesn't mean you can't appreciate and encourage your child whenever you see her flourish or succeed. It just means that you're not willing to manip- ulate. Children fare much better when a caring adult acknowl- edges and comments on their efforts. So feel free to revel in the joy and achievement of your child. Just don't be a driving judgmental force. Loving, thoughtful, and supportive interactions between you and your child will allow her to develop passion for the things she loves.

Advice from an Expert

Praising and rewarding are deeply ingrained habits, particularly as that's how most of us were raised and educated. It may take practice to replace them with appreciation and acknowledgment, but the latter feels more fulfilling, and can bring you and your child closer. Children can certainly be made to do what they don't want or love, by offering them approval, praise or other rewards. But this does not make them happy. Happiness can only be derived from doing what is intrinsically rewarding to us, and this does not require others' applause. Do we want kids to become reward-addicts, crowd-pleasers, and recognition-seekers, or do we want them to be self-motivated, faithful to themselves, following their own interests? If the latter is true, then the way is not to praise them but to appreciate them.

Children are born with an enormous desire to learn. They also have an innate capacity for honesty, empathy and considerateness. These qualities come forward as a result of our guidance, our role modeling, and our appreciation. Rewards and praise for "good behavior" or "good performance" simply get in the way.

—Dr. Robin Grille, *Parenting for a Peaceful World*

The following, adapted from the "Rewards and Praise: The Poisoned Carrot," by Dr. Robin Brille, is a list of recommendations of things to do instead of using praise.

1. Focus the child on her own joy in achieving.

Self-enjoyment fuels learning. When you see your child engaging in some activity, encourage and support her by saying, "You look like you're having a good time" or "How did it feel to do that?" or "It's cool that you tried that. You must be happy with yourself!"

2. Help him self-evaluate.

Try asking your child about how he thinks he did: "How do you like your painting?" or "Do you like how your castle of blocks turned out?"

3. Ask about her experiences.

If your child tells you she was her teacher's helper at school, you could ask, "How do you feel about that?" or "Did you enjoy helping, or were you nervous?" It's important to enrich your relationship with your child by showing interest in her feelings and experiences.

4. Use "I" statements, instead of labeling the child.

When you express your true feelings, your child feels the authenticity of your comment. For instance, "I" statements, such as "I like the outfit you're wearing!" or "I love how you hit the ball out of the field!" are more supportive than statements that label the child, such as "What a good ball player you are!" or "Gee, you're a great dresser." Avoid "Good boy for eating your entire meal!" Instead say, "Thanks for finishing your meal; you must have been hungry." Focus on your feelings, not on the label. "I" statements keep you from holding power over your child. They help create a close bond and connection between the two of you while not interfering with the child's experience of himself.

5. Comment on the behavior, not on the person.

Show interest and acknowledgment. If your child shows you a clay sculpture she made at school, instead of saying "What a good artist you are!" you could tell her how much you enjoy her art. Tell her what in particular you like about the sculpture—for example, the color and design, the cool eyes, how carefully she carved her name on the side.

DEALING WITH TANTRUMS

Children have tantrums because they have an innate, natural desire to be persistent and successful at everything they do, and their physical and emotional skills have developed more quickly than their ability to communicate. Children can also get very angry when they aren't able to experience their full autonomy and don't quite have the skill to express frustration. The older pre-schooler may have a tantrum as a misguided attempt to express himself.

Tantrums are a part of normal child development. Nonetheless, a tantrum is an emotional outburst of human feelings that, once it has been calmed, deserves your attention, validation, and guidance. Parents can actually play an active role in the prevention of this type of outburst by listening and acknowledging. It is also our job to provide a place for our children to let loose emotionally while feeling safe and secure.

The two types of tantrums we often see are frustration tantrums and attention-seeking tantrums. We've all seen the attention-seeker; she's sly and will do anything to get her way. She may get into the cookie jar after you've said no, and throws a fit if you try to correct her behavior. You'll need to set limits and walk away. In contrast, the frustration tantrum requires a helping hand and empathy. A child who is trying to fix a toy or put his jacket on by himself may spin out of control from sheer frustration. Getting angry or laughing at the outburst, no matter how funny it may look, will not help. Some of the best times to bond with your child are when he is in the midst of an emotional upheaval. Comfort your child and offer to assist him by saying, "Daddy is here; how can I help, honey?" Encourage your child to put words to his feelings. Do not ignore a frustration tantrum.

The following are some techniques that have worked for me and other parents I know.

Dealing with Attention-Seeking Tantrums

1. Plan ahead.

In advance, inform your child of what you expect. "Mommy needs to go shopping, but afterwards we can go get burgers and milkshakes. I know it's hard to shop with Mommy, but I really need your help."

2. Verbalize and empathize.

"You're mad at Mommy because I won't let you get down out of the stroller. I'm sorry it's taking so long; we're almost at the car."

3. Remain calm.

If your child gets physically out of control, calmly pick him up and go to the car. Let him know you're there to help and that you'll wait for him to calm down. Do not engage in conversation, threaten, or physically lash out.

4. Ignore it.

This is only an option if you're at home. If you feel your child is trying to get your attention and none of your other responses have worked, you can respectfully ignore the tantrum. Be sure you're nearby, but act as though you're engaged: wash dishes, check e-mail, or read. Don't get drawn into the tantrum or start arguing. You'll only fuel the fire.

If your child's tantrum is overly loud or disruptive, you can walk away and say, "This is hurting my ears. I need to leave the room." When she's quieting down you can say, "I'll be here when you're ready. I can hold you when you calm down" or "Would you like me hold you now?" Sometimes just acknowledging that it's hard when we don't get our way may be incentive enough for your child to stop the tantrum.

In the heat of either kind of tantrum, never engage in power struggles. The more you try to control your child, the more resistant he'll be. Before taking action, be sure you've checked if there are any unmet needs that drive the tantrum. If you were in emotional distress, the last things you'd want from the ones you love are rejection and abandonment. Respect and guidance will go a long way with your temper tantrum prevention efforts. A child's true sense of well-being is derived from your unconditional love and kindness.

Using Puppets or Stuffed Animals to Gain Cooperation

Because at this age their imaginations are flourishing, children are more apt to take instruction from one of their favorite stuffed toys than from their parents. You can use this to your advantage. I have a family favorite plush rhino that I pretend to make talk when I feel the boys may possibly resist cleaning up their room. I have the rhino say, "Boys, your mom has your bath ready, and you need to clean up so she doesn't turn into cranky mommy." The boys laugh as the rhino helps them clean up.

WHEN YOUR CHILD ACTS OUT IN PUBLIC

Sometimes we need to guide children in public when emotions are running high—there's nothing worse than a big power struggle on display for all the world. Say you're in the market and your child becomes resistant and defiant, or you're at a play date and your child is being pushy and bossy. If you find yourself angry, embarrassed, and impatient, take your child aside, out of the public view, to discuss the situation and how to correct it. Disciplining children in public can humiliate, embarrass, and anger them. And with an audience, your child knows how vulnerable you both are. Exerting too much control over your child and the situation will only bring on more defiance.

Here are some better ideas:

- Take your child aside, get down at her eye level, and softly explain what you see: "I see that you're frustrated that I won't let you open food here."

- Ask, "How can I help fix things?" If your child is under three years old, she probably won't be able to come up with something appropriate—offer empathy, encouragement, and a plan. If your child is four or older, she may be able to help with a plan. Always speak matter-of-factly and let her know you're willing to help and what you expect of her.

- Acknowledge her feelings and set up a plan so everyone's needs are considered.

Remember, the more force and control you use, the more resistant and difficult your child will be. Children tend to be more cooperative when we set the expectations ahead of time. Preparation and prevention are the keys to pleasant public outings with children.

Here's a formula to remember:

1. Address your child's feelings first.
2. State expected behavior.
3. Let your child know how you will help.

ANNOYING BEHAVIORS THAT ARE PART OF NORMAL DEVELOPMENT

Toddler behaviors that may seem utterly annoying may just be your child's natural way of growing into his ever-expanding mind—which is filled with excitement and endless possibilities.

Toddlers are curious, stubborn, strong willed, and highly exploratory. You should allow your child time every day for free play both indoors and out. Give him opportunities to try new things that are challenging and intriguing. Talk with your child about his feelings, and empathize.

Toddlers are also learning about their role in the world and what capabilities they have. They love to resist requests, run away, try to do everything their way, and say "No!" This can be frustrating for parents, but there's no need for strict discipline or harsh requests.

If you find that your toddler is always frustrated, reevaluate your daily activities. Do you have enough physical time, quiet time, and activities that challenge your child's mental and physical abilities? Children need to regularly learn new tasks—when children learn and master new tasks, they spend less time feeling frustrated.

The following are some basic issues that come up frequently.

Biting

Biting is one of the most challenging behaviors to deal with in young children. Children's bites can break the skin, which in turn can cause an infection, so you need to see biting behavior as a safety issue and intervene immediately.

Biting is common among toddlers and children who have limited vocabulary or poor impulse control. Sometimes toddlers have pent-up energy or are filled with excitement, and they choose biting as a way to express it. Also it could be that they're teething, and the biting is a way to release pain. Or they may get a kick out of the strong reaction their biting elicits. Most often the biter is frustrated and does not know what else to do.

For example, he may be involved in an activity that is too difficult for him, or the environment may be overstimulating. A child may be angry because he wants a particular toy. Because the child does not have the language skills to express his frustration, he resorts to biting.

Ways to Eliminate the Biting

- If the child does bite, immediately remove her from others. Tend to the victim, mend, hug, and kiss. Explain to the biter that biting hurts others and that it's "not okay." Continue to say, "Mama helps. No biting. Get me next time. Mama helps."
- Provide developmentally appropriate activities for the child.
- Provide more toys to eliminate the fighting.
- Tell the child to say no instead of biting when he's upset.
- Keep an eye on the biter so that you can learn to predict when biting may occur.

Hitting

You'd think that any parent dropping his child off at my house for a play date would feel that his kid has nothing to be worry about. After all, I'm a child behavior specialist, right?

Think again.

Not that long ago, my three-year-old had a buddy over to play, and they got into a pushing and yelling exchange that quickly escalated into a hitting match. I know that my son is very explosive when he doesn't get his way, so if there's a play date, everyone needs to stay close by to direct problematic behavior if it arises.

My eight-year-old was playing near his little brother and his buddy, who was four years old. When the two little guys started pushing, pulling, and hitting (what a sight to see in *my home*!), I broke up the fight, separated both very angry boys, and was going to go through the cool-down method with each one alone. As I was giving my three-year-old the "rules for playing with others" talk (much like Jillian's mom did in the Barbie scenario), I heard my son's four-year-old buddy talking with my eight-year-old.

The four-year-old said, "Is your mom going to hit me now?"

My older son said, "No, we don't punish in our home. She'll ask you what you did that was wrong and what you'll do next time. That's it; don't worry."

My heart was so warmed. What my son said was true. We don't punish. We set limits, empathize, and give tools for future play date success.

When Your Child Hits You When working to prevent your child from hitting anyone, the first thing to nip in the bud is his hitting you, his parent. Here's how it goes:

1. Tell your child, "No hitting. It's not okay." Hold his hands down if he continues to hit.

2. Say what you see: "I see you're mad at Daddy because it's time to go, but we don't hit."

3. Encourage your child to use his words or stomp his feet. Let your child know it's okay to be mad and even to express it, but never with his hands. You can say, "Use your words when you're mad." Further explain, "Next time you can tell me you're mad instead of hitting. Hitting hurts, and it's not okay."

4. After your child has calmed down you can say, "I know you get frustrated when you really want something and Daddy doesn't give it to you, but you may never hit."

5. Ask what he'll do next time: "Next time Daddy makes you mad, what will you do?"

6. Say, "We're always here to help you, especially when you're mad or need help. Thank you."

7. If he continues to hit, lead him to a cool-down time. Once he has regrouped, try these same steps again.

When a Child Hits Another Child Because hitting usually is a spontaneous act, we need to keep an eye on kids who we know have poor impulse control. In my case, my older son is calm and rarely lashes out if he is mad at another child. My three-year-old, however, needs close supervision, as he has a hostile temperament. Never minimize aggressive behavior. Hitting, pushing, and all acts of cruelty should be tended to immediately. When children begin to hit,

1. Tell them, "Hitting is not okay." Stop the hitting by removing the children from each other.

2. Ask the children what is going on: "I see you're very upset, but we don't ever hit or push. Can you tell me what's going on or why you're mad?"

3. Encourage them to use their words or stomp their feet—let them know that it's okay to be mad and even to express it, but never with their hands. Say, "Use your words when you're mad. Hitting hurts, and it's not okay."

4. After they've calmed down you can say, "I know you get frustrated when you don't get what you want, but you may never hit."

5. Remind them always to get an adult when their words don't work.

6. Ask them, "The next time you're mad, what will you do?" We hope they'll say, "Use my words or get a grown-up to help." If they don't have a solution, then brainstorm with them.

7. Wrap up with "Grown-ups are always here to help, especially when you're mad or need help. I trust you won't hit again."

8. If a child hits again, have her sit with you for a thinking or cool-down time.

Running Away

At any given moment, your child can take off and run out into a potentially dangerous situation. Here are some gentle tips for keeping your little one safe from harm:

- Set the expectation before you go out: "We are going to the park. No running away from Mama."

- When you get to your destination, plan some time for your child to run around to release some energy.
- While at home or in the yard if you have one, practice saying "Stop" with your child, and let her know that when you are out and say, "Stop," her body needs to stop.
- Always supervise your child no matter where you are.
- If your child begins to take off, catch up and let him know that you need to keep him close. Don't get angry; running is normal for this stage of development.
- Let her know that if she can't refrain from running off, she can either hold your hand or go in the stroller and have a snack.

Some people believe that this is the one type of scenario in which spanking is permitted. It is not! Spanking doesn't stop children from running into the street; it only makes them resent the spanker. You want your child to have a healthy and realistic fear of the dangers of running away or into traffic. Explain in a serious tone that you care and that you'll protect him by teaching him how to stay safe. Ask for his cooperation and then encourage his good listening skills. When you guide and communicate with your child instead of punishing him, you build trust—and trust breeds responsible kids.

TEACHING TODDLERS AND PRESCHOOL-AGE KIDS TO SHARE

Parents want their children to be kind and to share when playing with their friends. When your child refuses to share her toys, she isn't really being selfish—she's just acting her age. Sharing is a skill that is developed over time. In the meantime, struggles over toys will be common.

If your child does have a problem sharing and is two years old or younger, diversion and redirection will be the most effective strategies. Children learn how to share from their parents and their siblings. They pay attention to your actions, and they will follow your lead. So if you share, they'll eventually learn to share. Play next to your child and get him accustomed to sharing with you. Share toys, your food, or any other items that are safe for him to explore.

If your child is three years or older and you want to avoid tantrums over sharing, let your child put away a few of his favorite playthings before his friends arrive. Tell him these are toys he doesn't have to share. Let your child know that the toys that are left out are for everyone.

Another way to go is to let your child enjoy his toy before you ask him to hand it over to a friend. If a child is instructed to share before he's had an opportunity to enjoy his toy, it's possible that he'll resent the concept of sharing. But if he's had a chance to satisfy his own curiosity, he's more likely to be willing to take turns. We can help our kids develop positive perceptions of toys, sharing, and taking turns if we don't insist that they be the first to sacrifice.

It can be helpful to teach your child things to say that encourage sharing. Here are some basics:

"Can I have a turn?"
"When you're done, may I use it?"
"Would you like a try?"
"Can you share?"

Never punish a child for not sharing, and don't make a big deal out of it. You don't want sharing to become a power struggle. When your child doesn't share, you can step in and speak for her; once again you are modeling compassion and a behavior that you'd like your child to display.

If, for example, your son has left his toy sitting unused in the sandbox, but then grabs it away from another child who has picked it up, you can say to the other child, "I'm sorry he grabbed the shovel. He was excited to use it today. Would you like it when he is done?" Then you can say to your son, "Aaron, please get Mommy's help when you need a toy. Grabbing is not okay. I will always help."

Children like to be understood, and over time will trust your words and model your caring, sharing behaviors.

PLAYGROUND ETIQUETTE

There are things you can do if your child is aggressive and doesn't want to play cooperatively with other children. Try to follow the steps here the next time your child has to let someone else have a chance on the swing or won't budge to let others go down the slide.

1. Acknowledge your child's feelings: "You like the swing. You don't want to get off. Is this your favorite thing to do at the park?"

2. Make an observation: "You like it so much that you don't want to share."

3. Reflect: "How do you think the other kids feel not being able to have a turn?"

4. Ask for help: "What can we do to make these sad kids feel better?"

You want to have control *with* your children, not over them. The best way to teach children how to do the right thing is by modeling the behavior yourself.

If your child is unwilling to share her sand toys or ball at the park, then ask her if she'd be willing to leave her toys at home the next time you venture out. No need to create heated scenarios; we all know that kids who play at the park will find your child's toys very interesting, so preparing your child for this is key! Another option is to ask your child to bring the toys that she's *willing* to share—this way you won't be caught in the inevitable power struggle on your park play day.

Tips on Getting Dirty

It's OK to get dirty. Don't worry. Kids don't have to be spotless at all times!

Did you know that by providing your children the opportunity to play outdoors, you increase their self-reliance and cooperation with others? Outdoor play also reduces stress and acting out. Rocks, sand, mud, twigs, and water all make for great outdoor fun. Children can label, classify, and experiment with the elements of nature. Adventures in nature piques enthusiasms and joy—so let your kids get down and dirty where they learn, live, and play.

COMMON EARLY CHILDHOOD FEARS

It's seems second nature for us to deny our children's fears when they're afraid—after all, we're here to protect them. We know there are no such things as monsters. To children, however, fear of the unknown is natural, and those monsters hiding under the bed are for real. When your child turns two, things that didn't cause fear before can suddenly frighten him. My neighbor said, "My kids use to watch *Lion King* when they were two and had no fears, but now that they're four, they're terrified to see it."

Children of all ages experience fears, and some fears can persist into adulthood. The most effective way to help children deal with fear is through support and empowerment. Get to know your child and all the fear-inducing areas of her life. Denying or minimizing them will only make your child feel unsupported.

A child's imagination grows with her, and sometimes it includes scary things.

Toddlers' Fears

Toddlers may fear the dark, thunder and lightning, loud noises, animals, strangers, or separation. My niece had real fears of falling into the potty or going down the bathtub drain.

The biggest fear for this age group is being separated from loved ones. Toddlers' anxiety about separation is actually an indication of growth. It's easy to pass a baby off to another person because baby simply doesn't understand the world around her yet, and she seems pretty content most of the time. However, a budding toddler is beginning to sense that the world looks, smells, and feels different as she enters into new stages of development. For a toddler, things come and go, which at times include Mommy and Daddy. Separation anxiety can persist all the way through the preschool years.

Older Children's Fears

Four-year-old kids may fear loss of a parent or loss of control. It's not uncommon for young children to develop a fear of swimming, making new friends, or having to adapt to new situations. Children who are five have fears that are concrete or real: fear of getting hurt, public embarrassment, rejection, animals, the dark, death, or separation from Mom or Dad.

Sometimes children need to master a task first before letting go of the fear. A few years back, my son was very reluctant to learn how to ride a bike. He was so frustrated when he couldn't do it right away, and it embarrassed him to be seen trying and failing. With a little encouragement and a lot of support, he slowly gave it a chance, on his own timetable.

You can support your child of any age by normalizing his fears. Try using statements like these:

> "I see you're not happy in the pool. Let's get out, and you tell me when you're ready."
> "Wow, there are lots of new kids here. You don't know who to play with yet."

When a child is young, it's important to respond to his fears in a positive, supportive manner.

What to Do When Fears Are Present

1. Show respect. Never discount or minimize your child's experience or view her fears as silly or nonexistent.
2. Understand that your child will outgrow most fears.
3. Allow your child to gradually work through the fear by honoring her perception and letting her talk about it.
4. Be aware of the variety of fears children experience at different ages.

If you find that your child's fears have become unmanageable, impair family well-being, or interfere with school, get a referral from your pediatrician for a family therapist. Keep in mind that some fear is good. Children should have a healthy sense of caution. Strange people, unknown dogs, or tricky situations can be dangerous—and we want our children to trust their own instincts.

DINING OUT WITH YOUNG CHILDREN

Most families take their young children out for a meal every now and then, but there are some families who wouldn't dare to take on such a daunting task. It can be done, though, and it's a good learning experience for everyone.

Take your kids to restaurants. The more they go out, the quicker they'll learn what's expected and how to dine out with social grace. It may be challenging at first, so start with little cafés and family-friendly diners. If your children are picky eaters, make sure before you go that there's something they can order on the menu. Also, if your kids are ravenous when they walk into the restaurant, they may become overly cranky and refuse to eat anything. Most restaurants will customize food for children.

Make sure your little diner knows what's expected before you get to the restaurant. Proper restaurant behavior generally includes using quiet, indoor voices and sitting at the table. The goal is to not disturb other diners and to make sure that your child understands what is expected. If meltdowns begin to happen, then it's time to leave. But don't give up. Even after a disaster, try again.

Prepare Your Children for Dining Out

- Tell your children what you expect of them before you go.
- Clearly explain restaurant rules before you get there.
- Dine at kid-friendly restaurants.
- Bring a "restaurant toy bag" filled with small toys, workbooks, and little animals.
- Dine out early so that the restaurant's not too crowded and the children don't get hungry and cranky.

My husband and I decided to try a family-friendly Italian restaurant and thought we could take our two-year-old with us for the first time. Ha! As he wiggled under the table, jumped in the booth, and downright refused to eat by saying loudly, "NO, MAMA!" I calmly said to my husband, "Honey, I think I need to take this bambino to the car; please pack up my dinner."

My seven-year-old sat quietly, watching the whole thing go down. I wouldn't be surprised if he, too, becomes a shrink when he gets older. As I was wrangling my energetic toddler, my seven-year-old said, "Mom, how can you teach other people about children, when you can't handle your own?"

Out of the mouths of babes. His words remind me of good advice for all parents: we need to regroup before we let our anger set in. If you find yourself being impatient and impulsive, count to ten, calm down, and remove your child from the public arena.

TODDLER TOOTH CARE AND THE FIRST VISIT TO THE DENTIST

By the time your baby reaches six months old, you can begin to clean his gums with a wet baby washcloth. Before he turns two, his back molars will have come in; you can then switch to a soft-bristle infant or toddler toothbrush. Because tots like to walk around and brush, it's a good idea to start out with the triangle safety brush.

Letting Them Brush Themselves

As soon as you begin to brush your child's teeth, you'll notice his desire to brush them himself. Our dentist says that parents should always assist with one of the brushings until a child is ten years old because the back molars need a parent's help. Brush your teeth while he's doing his, but be sure to check and see if his are clean.

If he resists your help, tell your child that you promised the dentist that you'd help out. Show him that he "missed a spot" and finish the brushing. That way you'll have done a complete cleaning. Both my boys fussed when it was time to brush—it is surely a challenge, but the job has to get done to avoid tooth decay. Our dentist tells our kids that if they don't brush well, the "plaque bugs" will grow on their teeth. My kids think that's pretty gross, so if I mention the plaque bugs, they get brushing!

If you have a resistant brusher, it may help to get her a toothbrush with her favorite character on it. You can also let your child have different brushes so that she can choose the one she's in the mood for. I love to use the electric toothbrush with my boys because it really removes the plaque. We've had Buzz Lightyear, Wall-E, you name it and we've used it—anything to help the kids keep up good dental hygiene.

First Visit to the Dentist

Parents want to know when their child's first dental visit should be. Some pediatric dentists recommend that children come in as young as one year old (or when they get a few new teeth). It's a good idea to prepare your young child for her first dental visit. Here are some tips to keep the visit calm, cool, and fun:

1. Call the office in advance and see what their procedures are. (Do they let babies or toddlers sit on Mommy's lap? Do they give a sticker or prize afterward, or have a DVD cartoon playing on the ceiling?)
2. Let your child know that you're going to visit the dentist and that everybody goes to the dentist.
3. Tell him that the dentist will lean him back in a cool movable chair, count his teeth, show him how to clean them, and give him a brand-new toothbrush and maybe even a cool toy from the treasure box.
4. Play "dentist" at home to encourage her to view dental appointments as fun and exciting.

If parents are cheery and upbeat when taking their kids to the dentist, there's a good chance that their children will adopt the same attitude!

POTTY TRAINING NATURE'S WAY

Have you ever met a normally developed adult who wasn't potty trained? I haven't. Don't worry that if you take a laid-back approach, you'll still be changing your child's diapers in elementary school. Bladder control is a physiological function and not something that can be controlled with behavioral remedies.

Rewarding children with stickers, charts, and toys doesn't speed up the process. Demanding that your child use the potty only brings on more control issues. Potty battles are disruptive to a good parent-child relationship. You didn't reward your child for walking for the first time, so why would you reward her for bladder control? It takes the average child at least twelve months to master this task. Girls typically begin to use the potty at two-and-a-half, boys around their third birthday.

When your little one turns fifteen months, you can buy a cute potty or potty-top seat. Bring it outside during the warmer months and let your child play diaperless. Children need to see where their pee-pee comes from. If they're in a diaper, it's hard for them to make the connection. If they pee in the bush or on the grass, you can say, "There's your pee." Don't get too excited; just be matter-of-fact.

You want to expose children to the potty on a regular basis over the long run, so don't rush them. All children really need is to see you, their siblings, or their peers using the bathroom. Most likely they'll find joy in trying to go potty. Isn't this low-stress method preferable to forcing a developmental process that your kid has no or little control over?

Children tend to learn to use the potty on their own when they're in a supportive, noncontrolling environment. Kids who attend preschool tend to become potty trained earlier because they get to see their peers use the bathroom. Modeling and exposing your child to the elements of using the potty are all you need to do. Relax and enjoy your child, because tomorrow she'll be going off to college, and you'll kick yourself for not savoring all the wonderful stages.

One final note: there's no specific age that is considered optimal for training; however, if your child is not using the potty by age four, consult with your pediatrician.

PROBLEMS WITH SLEEPING

By the time children are age five, they've spent half their lives asleep. Biologically the body and brain need as much sleep as possible for children to focus, handle their moods, and perform. Sleep studies have shown that sleep deprivation problems can start even at toddler age. Lack of sleep or trouble sleeping can make it difficult for young children to concentrate; they also tend to lose control of their emotions, thus leaving them susceptible to frequent power struggles that make it hard for them to cooperate with others. Children of all ages will act out or be difficult to manage if they haven't had sufficient sleep.

How Much Sleep Does Your Child Need?

One year old:	13 hours
Two years old:	12–15 hours (includes nap)
Three years old:	11–14 hours (includes nap)
Four years old:	10–13 hours (includes nap)
Five years old:	10–12.5 hours (no nap)

There are many stressors that can affect your child's sleep. Take a look at your child's day to see if there are patterns or possibly a one-time event that's causing some tension. When a child feels that his sense of safety or security is threatened, he may be at risk for having escalated stress hormones, which leaves him unable to get a good night's sleep. Parental stress, separation from a loved one, overstimulation, upsetting events, overscheduling, a competition the next day, or any schedule changes can affect your child's coping skills. As when dealing with tantrums, you need to see what the underlying daily problem is that's causing your child to miss sleep. Once you know the culprit, you can relax and make efforts toward addressing the cause, ensuring that for the sake of her growth and family harmony, your child gets her much-needed sleep.

How Lack of Sleep Can Cause Misbehavior

Does your child get keyed up instead of drowsy when he should be tired? Does he have tantrums out of nowhere, or have overly strong emotional reactions to normal, everyday issues? Does he hit, constantly grab snacks from the cabinet, or regularly display frenzied behavior? Overly tired children can't appropriately balance their physical and emotional world. Well, don't feel alone, because there are many parents whose children have sleep problems, and I'm one of them. It takes a concentrated effort on my part to ensure that my youngest son gets enough sleep, for without it, he simply can't function.

Just as you can't force a horse to drink water, you can't force kids to sleep. But you can create a cozy environment that's conducive to sleep. Both adults and children need their rest, and what better way for them to get it than by snuggling up with each other in a dim room while reading a peaceful story?

Things You Can Do to Ensure That Your Child Gets Enough Sleep

- Children who nap have fewer behavior problems. If your child is less than four years old, be sure that she has a midday nap on a regular schedule.

- Make after-dinner playtime a relaxing time. Too much activity close to bedtime can keep children awake.

- Set a regular time for bed each night and stick to it.

- Establish a relaxing bedtime routine; for example, give a bath and read stories.

- Set the bedroom temperature so that it's comfortable—not too warm and not too cold.

- Make sure that your child's sleep environment is snug, cozy, and dark. If necessary, use a white-noise machine and a nightlight. Keep the noise level low.

When Your Child Resists Naptime

Young children need to nap daily. Most children would benefit from maintaining a nap routine until they're five years old, but that's not always the case. You may need to push your child's naptime to later in the day. I know that both my boys napped fine on their own until they turned two, at which point I started lying down with them until they fell asleep. Napping was and is very important in our family, for without it, the inevitable 6:00 P.M. meltdown occurs.

Some children just aren't efficient daytime sleepers and won't nap after they're three. If your child gives up her nap, be sure to put her to bed early enough that she gets her full thirteen hours of required sleep. My eight-year-old gave up his naps at three; however, he's mild mannered and can stay calm and rested the entire day without a meltdown—unlike my strong-willed three-year-old, who still needs his nap no matter what!

If your child simply doesn't sleep after you've tried to rest with her for thirty minutes, get out one of her books and continue the "rest time" so that your child has at least a quiet time each day. Dim the lights, get into bed, and read soothing stories.

THE SCOOP ON TV AND DVD TIME

Babies and toddlers learn best from interacting with you and the world around them, not from TV or DVDs. Plain and simple: babies don't need TV. Babies and toddlers thrive on touching, feeling, and experiencing life through uninhibited exploration of the real, three-dimensional world.

That's not to say that you can't use a DVD for a limited amount of time (fifteen to twenty minutes) to keep your toddler occupied while you get dinner ready. However, I encourage you to review any programming you plan on exposing your child to and make sure the content is age appropriate. I know that as parents we certainly aren't perfect and may at times rely on DVDs to make parenting more manageable; however, the American Academy of Pediatrics recommends no TV or DVDs for children under two years of age. The Canadian Pediatric Society believes that once children turn one year old, moderate programming or DVD viewing is acceptable.

Expert Advice on Screen Time

Media are here to stay, in case you have not figured that out yet, we live our lives consuming media every day, and quite a lot of it. Media is not inherently bad. Media can have bad content. Bad people are out there as characters in a movie and as predators online. Media have become our village storytellers. But this is not all bad. For as many dumb stories that are told on television, I think there are probably just as many told in books. It is important to remember that media have a lot to offer. Good stories. Good morals. Lessons. Knowledge. It is not possible, nor is it really favorable, to completely unplug your kids. To do so would put them at a disadvantage in today's plugged-in world. Rather, let them stay plugged in, but not all the time, and not with the unsavory elements that are offered in each of the major types of media. As your kids get older, educate them about media. Inoculate them so that when they are plugged in they shed off the bad messages and bad potential influences and maximize the good.

—David Dutwin, PhD, *Unplug Your Kids*

The real goal here is to see TV for what it is: purely entertainment. I feel some of the media hype around why parents shouldn't expose their young child to DVDs or TV is to ensure that parents don't misuse TV by using it as a replacement for human interaction and real-life learning moments, or as a distraction from spending time with family. When the kids get older, properly monitored screen time, including broadcast TV and Internet research, can be a valuable educational tool, not to mention its potential for healthy social networking. A special note: I may be a bit lax on DVD viewing because I myself like watching them, and let my kids do it too. However, I want to caution parents about allowing their child to have a television set in her bedroom. All media, computers included, should be in an open space or family room where you can properly monitor content and time spent viewing. The more electronics you allow in a separate place, the less time you will spend together as a family.

THE GO-TO MOM'S QUICK AND NIFTY TIPS

Encourage Sensitivity Through Interaction

Give inanimate objects (stuffed animals) or living creatures (family pet) a real voice when difficult situations arise. Kids love to know that the things in their world understand them.

When my kids chase our cat I say, "Monkey cat told me she's scared when you chase her. Ask her yourself." When the kids ask her, I speak as the cat, and even though I'm standing right there, they don't seem to see me. I kneel down to our cat and use a silly kitty voice: "Please don't chase me. I like when you pet me, but I want to hide when you chase me." The kids listen to her. Young children believe in fantasy, so use it while you can.

Rotate Toys

You're probably tossing out toys left and right because toy clutter is mind-boggling, but because children play with toys differently

(continued)

during their stages of development, don't be so quick to toss out a toy they've lost interest in.

Your two-year-old may play with the barn's doors and stomp the horse around. However, when he turns four, dramatic play is in full effect, and he might have the farmer talk and figure out ways to have the horse pull the hay.

To get the most out of your child's toys, store their favorites away or put them on a rotation schedule so that when you bring them out again, they spark new interest. Store toys away for three to five months at a time. You'll be pleasantly surprised at your child's response when you bring them back out.

Use Fun Ways to Get Your Toddler to Sit Still for a Nail Trimming

For some reason children just don't want to sit still for grooming, and I don't know why, because I truly look forward to getting my nails done!

Here's an innovative way to get your child to sit still for a nail trimming: add some adventure and drama to the process. It works almost every time! Tell your child you need to rescue the hippo and rhino and eight other animals from their toes. As you clip each nail say, "There! The rhino is out! Whew!" or "Oh, I see a giraffe in this toe!" Most likely she'll sit for all ten piggies because she can't wait to hear what kind of animal is rescued next!

5

As Your Child Advances in Development, So Do the Challenges

Guiding Your Four- to Seven-Year-Old

> Children misbehave when they feel discouraged or powerless.
>
> —Kathryn J. Kvols, *Redirecting Children's Behavior*

You may think that because your child is becoming a big kid, all her emotional impulses should now be fully formed and under her control. Think again. Children from four to seven years old are more in tune with their environment and how the world works, and are beginning to reveal their true unique temperament. At this age they are savvy enough to make some of their own decisions based on how they think and feel, without our intervention. Their personality is unfolding right before our eyes. However, their social-emotional development is something that we can't readily see or measure. Kids may grow into big bodies but pretty much have young hearts up until the end of grade school. It's imperative that we honor our child's innocence and naïveté until they show us that they no longer need our input. Our job as parents is to adjust to our children's emerging needs and to provide continual guidance and support.

By now you know what makes your child unique. For example, my eight-year-old son is very sensitive and compliant and needs opportunities to practice saying no. He also needs to learn to feel safe when asserting himself. My three-year-old, in rather stark contrast, is highly physical and emotionally charged. He needs us to help him feel more powerful and somewhat self-contained so that he doesn't have emotional explosions when distressed. We have to set firm boundaries with him—more than we do with our older son; we also must frequently prepare him in advance for potentially challenging situations, as he frequently acts on his first impulse. There is no such thing as one-size-fits-all parenting; we have to approach each of our kids differently.

No matter what your child's unique temperament, allowing him a healthy outlet for emotional expression is good parenting. Setting limits and being clear about what you expect set the stage for long-term cooperation and responsibility. But what about those times when you're at a loss for what to do—for example, when your child is resistant, extremely challenging, or defiant? Whether they're whiny, aggressive, or just sad, children will always need our intervention!

CRYING

Whenever I cried as a child, my parents told me to stop—that whatever I was crying over wasn't worth it. As a result of such parental constraint, I held back my tears for most of my young life. I was never allowed to process my feelings. All I knew was how to express myself in the most primitive ways: either through anger or sadness. Then, when I finally left home for college, I found myself crying continually for years to come. It was as though I needed to pour out eighteen years' worth of tears that had been bottled up inside. A part of me also had known all along that it was useful to cry, and now I was finally able to cry whenever I felt the urge.

If you let the air build up in a pressurized bottle, it eventually bursts. What parent wants that for their child? My children are very efficient criers—they do it well and often. At times I feel that they're making up for all those years of crying that *I* missed out on.

It's natural for parents not to want their children to cry, both because it is hard to see them in distress and because of the societal perception that crying is a form of weakness, of losing control. However, allowing your child to cry is okay and healthy, for crying serves many positives functions in early childhood and beyond. Babies cry because it's their basic form of communication. Preschoolers cry because they don't have the ability to tell us exactly what they're feeling emotionally. After a good cry, a child's in a better state to talk about what he's feeling. Love and support your crying child, even when you think that what she's crying about is silly or unimportant.

Helping a Child Cope When a Parent Leaves on a Trip

It's not easy for children when a parent goes away on a business trip. Children don't have the emotional vocabulary to express how they feel about being left behind. They may deal with the separation by withdrawing, showing sadness or anger, or acting out. Young children can find it a confusing experience when a parent comes and goes.

Use markers or crayons to make a travel calendar with your child to help her cope with the separation. Draw pictures of Dad on his trip and have your child mark off the days until he comes home.

Day 1: Daddy gets on an airplane.

Day 2: Daddy visits Grandma's.

Day 3: Daddy has a business meeting.

Day 4: Daddy flies home on an airplane.

As children get older, they eventually learn to express many of their feelings without tears. However, if they're not permitted to cry, they lose a golden opportunity to explore and master their internal world. Children will continue to shed tears for the rest of their lives when in physical and emotional pain, so prepare them to accept tears as healthy and normal. Teach your child to move through life's tough moments with strength and confidence—which at times may include a good cry.

SADNESS

Stressful or sad situations can cause worry or anxiety in children of this age. It's important to be aware of your children's feelings after a loss, separation, or major event that changes their lives. Moving, starting a new school, divorce, and death of a pet are all common reasons for children to become sad.

Our jobs as parents is to help children understand their sad feelings. For example:

- Allow your child to be sad. Everyone needs time to express grief. Don't be upset if your child shows strong emotions.

- Allow him to cry—crying is part of the grieving process and can help young children heal. Don't expect your children to be "brave" and tough at all times.

- Provide empathy. Let her know that sometimes you're sad and that you know how it feels. Talking and, more important, listening can help ease childhood sadness. Empathy bonds parent and child when times are emotionally difficult.

- Encourage your child to talk or draw pictures about his feelings. It's important for children to have outlets to help them explore how they feel.

- Be prepared for your child to regress to behaviors they'd outgrown—bed-wetting, separation anxiety, acting out, or thumb sucking.

It's important for children to understand that it's okay to feel sad and express their emotions. Also let them know that there are things they can do to help themselves feel better and that you're always there to help or talk to.

GOOD MANNERS AND SOCIAL GRACE

Children with good manners and courteous ways make themselves welcome in public places and are bound to impress the adults around them. These positive reactions reinforce for your child that the world can be a pleasant place with friendly people in it.

Teaching Kindness and Gratitude

The best way to teach your child good old-fashioned manners is to practice courteous behaviors yourself. If you say "please" and "thank you" to your child and to people in public, your child will do the same. Children learn best through role modeling, and if you show them respect, they naturally learn to respect others.

Model courtesy to others by lending a helping hand to the elderly, giving up your seat in public, and holding open the door for people. Your child is watching!

Children will learn the most about manners from watching you, but there are also a couple of other things that you can teach.

Teach the value of privacy. Define the word *private* so that when you use it, your child knows what you mean. Let him know that if he has questions about people, their physical appearance, ailments, or handicaps, he should ask you in private. Remind him not to invade people's personal space by staring or getting too much in their face.

Young children often innocently ask embarrassing questions that can leave you breathless and unprepared in the moment. Don't overreact, but don't ignore the situation either. One time in the drug store when my son was four years old, he loudly asked me, "Mommy, why are some people fat?" An overweight woman was standing a few feet way. I gasped, embarrassed, and pulled him in close to quiet him. Kneeling down I whispered, "I'll answer you when we get into the car, okay honey?"

Once in the car I continued our discussion and explained, "It's not polite to talk in public about how people look. It can hurt their feelings." I told him that if he ever has questions about people to always feel free to ask me—but in private, not in front of others.

Model apologizing, but don't force your child to give an insincere apology. Children usually are not sorry when they do something wrong. When an adult makes a child say, "I'm sorry," she's asking her child to be insincere. If a child chooses to say it on his own, it's authentic and heartfelt. When your child does something in public that you feel warrants an apology, you can apologize for the mishap. When my toddler would push someone, I'd say to the other child, "I'm sorry, sweetie, are you okay? My son is learning to share, and sometimes he pushes." I'd immediately talk with my son about never hitting or pushing. He might feel remorse in a few minutes or maybe a few days, but I knew he'd learn more from feeling sincere empathy and regret on his own schedule rather than one I forced on him. Children need to be guided and directed toward appropriate behaviors that you want them to adopt; you don't speed up the learning process by making them mechanically do or say things.

WHINY BEHAVIOR

Whining is a normal part of the four- to seven-year-old's life, and it's probably one of the most annoying behaviors for adults to encounter. Children whine for many reasons: they're tired, hungry, bored, or lonely, or they need a little love and attention. It's important to encourage children to reduce their whining when they're young; you don't want them to use whining as a form of communication as they get older.

Looking for patterns is key to curbing whining. Your child may whine if you take her on errands that are close to lunch or naptime, if you haven't heard her first request, or if she's overdressed and can't express her discomfort. When children wake up, they're often discombobulated, and whine because they're not fully awake. Don't take whining personally; just be patient and offer a healthy snack and love.

My oldest son was a whiner. Whenever he whined around me I'd say, "We have a no-whining rule in the house. The only place you may whine is in the privacy of your bedroom." That way he could close the door and whine all he wanted. However, I was caught off guard once. I was in his room putting some toys away, and he began to whine. The hairs stood up on the back of my neck, and I turned to him and said, "No whining. You need to leave the room and whine somewhere else." He kindly brought to my attention that I was in *his* room, which was indeed the only place he was allowed to whine! Got me on that one!

Tips on How to Help Stop the Whiny Behavior

First determine if your child is hungry, thirsty, tired, and physically uncomfortable or overstimulated—maybe too many people are around. Figure out the cause and meet your child's needs immediately. Sometimes just meeting a physical need will stop the whining. Remember, a toddler will whine because he doesn't know how he's feeling at the moment and may need your help. In contrast, a preschooler or older child may whine to cope with frustration about not getting his way.

Whatever the reason for the whining,

- Let your child know you can't understand what she's saying when she whines.

- Ask your child to use her regular voice.

- If she continues to whine, tell her, "When you use your regular voice, I'll listen, but when you whine, I can't hear what you're saying" or "If you feel a need to whine, please go to your room and do it there."

- Once she's back to using her regular voice, validate her current feelings and continue to listen. For example, "You're sad that your friends left the park early; what would you like to do now?"

- After that, the next time your child slips into whining, simply remind her of how you can hear her best. Once the whining ceases, a simple statement such as, "Thank you for using a regular voice this time," is appropriate. Further praise isn't necessary.

WEAPON AND SUPERHERO PLAY

Children from four to seven—boys in particular—often want to feel more powerful and bigger than they are. Children live in a world where grown-ups have all the power and control. For many children, weapon play is one of the ways they physically express their zest for life, process their fears, make themselves feel safe, and experiment with self-defense. There's nothing more empowering to a kid than to fend off the monsters or pirates that lurk around the corner.

This is a natural phase that should come after four or five years of age—unless there's an older sibling who's already exposed your child to the elements of *Star Wars* or Indiana Jones. Playing aggressively with toys or engaging in pretend weapon play allows children to process anger and other concerns they may have. If you have a child under the age of three who's obsessed with weapons, take a closer look at what the possible influences may be. Most children who feel empowered and powerful throughout the day don't have a desire to engage in constant weapon play.

Children shouldn't be exposed to violent influences through the media or from their peers. Exposing children to violent toys, programming, or video games desensitizes them to violence. Don't encourage this type of play with toddlers; they're simply too young to comprehend any of the concepts behind weapon use, war, and superhero play.

As children grow older, they begin to understand how weapons have played a part in our history. They may begin to ask questions about why people use guns and swords. It's best to keep your very young child engaged in real-life hero play by encouraging him to be a firefighter or carpenter who rebuilds fallen buildings. Once kids are older, their natural curiosity kicks in, and they'll be more equipped to safely engage in weapon play with their buddies.

Superhero and weapon play isn't all bad. This type of play makes it possible for kids to make distinctions between good and evil, right and wrong, power and powerlessness, good guys versus bad guys. The power and glory of superheroes are attractive to kids who feel they have few of these qualities. Superhero or weapon play is not harmful when it serves as an outlet for creative expression—or when it's safely used to solve personal emotional conflict.

Healthy Ways to Support Superhero Play

Here's how this type of play can be most beneficial for children who are five or older:

- State the rules, such as, "Use your words and don't hurt anyone or the things around you."
- Take opportunities to talk about how the bad guy could have made a better decision.

- Encourage kids to take turns so that everyone can be both the "good guy" and the "bad guy."
- Establish the rule that if one child wants to stop the game, it's okay.
- Give children power over fearful situations by providing them with firefighting props, doctor kits, and toy construction tools.
- Make sure children aren't exposed to real-life violence. Children need to spend less time with video games and TV and more time engaged in interactive and creative play.
- Put a time limit on the play or stop it all together if it's getting too aggressive.
- Make an agreement that if someone gets hurt or isn't playing safely, the game will have to stop.

Be sure your child has regular opportunities to feel responsible, needed, and valued. A child who feels important and who feels safe to express himself would never intentionally seek to hurt another. Dramatic play empowers children and offers them the perfect scenario to work out their values, conflicts, and identity.

BOSSY KIDS

No parent wants a bossy kid, but at some point your four- to seven-year-old may enter a "bossy phase." Bossy kids just may be emerging leaders testing their skills! Sometimes children come on too strong because they don't feel heard or valued. Sometimes children learn controlling behaviors from their older siblings, so in turn boss their friends around.

Pay attention to bossy behavior and don't hesitate to intervene.

Monitor Bossy Behavior

- Ask your child to speak kindly, and remind her that unkind words hurt people's feelings.

- Provide guidance. Coach your child on how to express her feelings and desires. Help her stand up for herself, and always let her know you are there to help.

- Know your child's friends. Consider their different temperaments and make efforts to prevent situations that you know might cause a flare-up of bossy behaviors.

- Teach your child to get a grown-up when he needs help.

- Always nurture and empathize with children in conflict. If your child is being bossy, listen and then privately bring to his attention that his strong demands may be the reason why some friends don't want to play with him. Brainstorm solutions to regain harmony. When the day is over, mention to your little one how well he treated his friends after the two of you had your talk. Let him know you appreciate it when he follows through and that someday when he's older, he'll make a good leader.

YELLING AND SCREAMING

Children are filled with boundless energy, which they may express in ways that are loud and hard on a parent's ears. Screaming and yelling obviously are ways for children to show either excitement or anger, but can become quite disrespectful if another's personal space is violated.

Screaming Because of Excitement

If your child is a habitual screamer, you'll need to make efforts to lower her pitch, volume, and tone when she is around others or indoors. Acknowledge her feelings and set limits: "You're very excited that Tara's here, but you need to lower your tone and use your indoor voice." Teach your child that yelling is for outside. When he raises his voice at home, get down on his level and explain the difference between indoor voices and outdoor voices.

Even if you have a high tolerance for noise, don't allow your child to be loud. Kids whose parents don't monitor their social behavior have kids who raise their voices anywhere and anytime they please. This is one of those important limits we need to set so that our kids learn to respect others and achieve good manners and social grace.

Yelling out of Anger

Many children who are screamers feel helpless and resort to this form of primitive behavior because they don't know what else to do. Or maybe you are a yeller, and they're just mimicking your style. I raise my voice, so it's no mystery why my three-year-old does too. I have to be very conscious of how I express my dissatisfaction around my kids; they're always watching. It's my job to help my son (and myself!) channel anger through productive and acceptable outlets.

When my son shouts in anger, I approach him and ask what's going on. I listen and validate his feelings: "You're mad because the truck door won't shut. That's frustrating." I don't jump to rescue him, but I offer help: "Can Mama help you? Show me." Sometimes he doesn't need my help, but my presence and understanding seem to de-escalate his anger. Once things are calm, I ask him, "Is it okay to scream when you're mad?" I encourage him to try alternative means of self-expression: "If you're mad, it's okay to say 'I'm mad!' but it's not okay to scream. It hurts our ears." I continue with, "When you're upset, I do hear you—there's no need to yell. I'm really here, and I will help."

SHYNESS

Shy children can find social situations very stressful. These children may be quite talkative in the privacy of their own homes but become insecure in the outside world.

At home, my older son is outgoing, rambunctious, articulate, and silly—however, in public he can barely look an adult in the eye or say hello to the school crossing guard. He was publicly shy as a toddler and still is at eight years of age.

It's quite commonplace for adults to say, "She's just shy; she'll grow out of it," which is essentially denying the shy child her experience. Research shows that some children do suffer from real social anxiety (which can show up as extreme shyness) and that minimizing it only makes it worse. Dr. Ward K. Swallow, the author of *The Shy Child: Helping Children Triumph over Shyness*, states, "Although we often think of shyness as a social handicap, shy children tend to grow up into sensitive, empathetic adults. They have such a rich internal world. They spend time analyzing why people do the things they do, and they have wonderful imaginations."

Most shy children are born that way. Their oversensitivity to new people and situations has been linked to genetics. Because shy children need a lot of encouragement, you'll find that planning social events or play dates will take extra preparation. There is no easy way to get a shy child to become more social. If you push too hard, your child will resist even more.

My son had a tendency to stay by my side the entire time at play dates and parties, so I had to set some ground rules about acceptable behavior in advance. On the way over, I'd say, "I know it's hard for you to warm up on play dates. You can stay with me for a while, but I want you to play with the other children at some point" or "No sitting on Mommy's lap the entire time."

Tips for Making Your Child Feel More Comfortable

- Prepare your child for new experiences.

- Listen patiently. You can say, "Feeling shy can be hard" or "Sometimes I need to warm up too."

- Try to role-play or make a game of acting out different scenarios with your child, such as meeting a new kid at school.

- Don't label your child as shy. Reframe your words and instead say, "You just need some time to warm up" or "I see you don't like it when people look at you."

- Let your child see that you view socializing as a fun part of everyday life.

- Be patient. Although helping your child feel at ease in new situations may take a little extra planning, the results will last a lifetime.

- Encourage your child to look adults in the eye when he is spoken to.

- Find a great preschool. Shy children can blossom in the right environment. Try to choose a program that has a low student-teacher ratio. Let the teacher know about your child's shyness.

- Never demand that your child become more bubbly or outgoing, and don't force social behaviors.

LYING

You may be alarmed the first time you hear that your child has lied. Don't worry. It's not unusual. Preschool children who lie usually don't have a serious problem. Sometimes they have a hard time distinguishing the difference between reality and fantasy. And boy, do they love to tell elaborate tales! A child who lies usually has a hard time looking you in the eye, so the lie won't be hard to see. Older children may lie because they fear their parent's reaction to the truth. If your child does lie, ask yourself if you're too hard on her when she does tell the truth.

Lying or making things up is most common in preschool children, who still have an amazing fantasy life and can't yet distinguish between right and wrong. Children may also lie to avoid being punished or because they're imitating adult behavior. Parents are the most influential role models for their children, so it's important that you curb your fibbing as well. Parents pass on values and morals to their children. Your child will learn honesty and dishonesty where he lives—in the home.

Here's what to do:

- Discuss the difference between make-believe and reality.
- Clearly define lying and telling the truth.
- Explain the importance of honesty in and out of the home.
- Offer alternatives to lying—for example, asking a grown-up for help, asking to borrow a toy instead of just taking it.

If you know your child has stolen something, yet she claims she didn't, you can say, "Sometimes kids want things so badly they take it, because they feel that no one will give it to them. Do you ever feel that way? Let's talk about this . . ."

When your child chooses to tell the truth after an incident of lying, let her know that you appreciate her effort. Also let her know that it's never okay to lie and that telling the truth right away is better than lying or stalling.

If your child develops a pattern of lying or is six or older and intentionally lies, seek professional help from a child or family counselor.

BED-WETTING

About 13 percent of six-year-olds and about 5 percent of ten-year-olds wet the bed. Don't be discouraged if your child wets the bed every night. It's a challenge that you and your child can overcome through patience and unconditional reassurance. Children under six years old do wet the bed; it's not abnormal or a cause for concern. However, if your child continues to wet the bed after the age of seven or eight, then consult with your pediatrician.

Nighttime bladder control is a capability dependent on physical development, so be assured that with support and guidance, your child will outgrow the bed-wetting and will eventually master dry nights. Don't hold unrealistic expectations for a quick change in a process over which your child has little or no control. The key to an easy transition is for you to be well informed about what your child can and can't do.

I strongly advise that you do *not* "teach your child a lesson" by making him change his bedding or sleep in wet clothes. One mother told me that if her son wet the bed, she was going to make him bring his wet sheet to school to show his first-grade classmates. I understood her frustration, but I explained the possible damage that such a punishment would do to her son. It is never okay to humiliate or punish a child for wetting the bed, no matter what his age. Not all children gain bladder control at the same time. Please be gentle and understanding if you have a child who still wets her bed.

Reasons Why Children Wet the Bed

- Their bladders have not fully matured. This lack of muscle strength is causing them to wet the bed.
- They are very deep sleepers and simply can't wake to empty their bladders in time.
- They have stresses brought on by a new baby, a divorce, transitioning into a new school or getting a new teacher, a death, a family crisis, or physical changes (such as diabetes).
- They are experiencing severe discipline, abuse, threats, or inconsistent caregiving, or they are living with parental yelling

and fighting. Sudden emotional instability can cause serious psychological strain.

- The kidneys of some children produce more urine than a normal-size bladder can hold.
- There's a hormone that causes the kidneys to slow their production of urine during the evening that only begins to develop when the child is between the ages of four to eight.

Ways to Help with Bed-Wetting

- Never punish, bribe, use rewards or sticker charts, or demand that your child stay dry during the night.
- Listen to the concerns of your child. Children rarely wet the bed on purpose. Take the time to listen to their fears and concerns.
- Assure your child that you're there to help and support him. Always be matter-of-fact so that he doesn't feel embarrassed or ashamed.
- Keep this issue private. There's no need to tell friends, teachers, or neighbors.
- Limit liquid intake before bed.
- Wake your child up in the middle of the night, before you go to bed, for one last bathroom visit. Some kids are very deep sleepers and can't wake on their own—getting them up will help them start the ritual.

See a doctor if your child abruptly starts to wet the bed; she may have a urinary tract infection or an underlying emotional problem. A lot of patience and a little knowledge can help you and your child understand and deal with bed-wetting.

CLEANING UP TOYS AND BELONGINGS

Cleaning up is not an instinctive activity or intuitive skill—although I may have some rare tidiness gene! Children don't need any encouragement to spread their toys around or to flick paint here and there, but cleaning up takes a little coaxing. This can be a lonely task for a social child and at times can feel like punishment or a never-ending chore.

There are some ways in which parents can begin to teach the value of cleanliness. First and foremost, be a tidy role model. This means you must model the behaviors you want to see in your child. Young children actually learn best through experience and not always through formal instruction. I don't have the magic formula, but I do have some helpful tips.

1. Young children love to be a part of team efforts, and they like to help, so enlist your child as your little helper. When he spills something or makes a mess, you can say, "I see you spilled. We'd better clean that up; want to help? Mommies always help kids, don't they?"

2. Have a place for everything: storage boxes, shelves, and cubbies. Soon your child will begin to remember where everything should go. Enlist puppets or use social play during cleanup times. Sing songs or make up silly rhymes as you put things away.

3. By age four or five, your child should know how to pick up by herself. If you encounter the "not-so-good listener," you can bring to her attention the natural consequence of not cleaning. You can say, "I know it's hard to clean up sometimes, but we've got to get to the park, and we can't leave these toys everywhere—you need to help pick up." Or if he asks, "Why does my room have to be clean?" have a discussion and ask him, "Why do you think it should be clean?" You'll find that he knows why.

It's not that children don't want to clean up alone or to complete the task, it's that they don't have the ability to focus for long periods when they're young. Cleaning a room can seem like a very big task to a little child—especially if she's by herself. You can offer some help and empathize by saying, "I know it's hard to clean a big mess; I can help if you like." Or say, "Do you think you need to get that many toys out next time you play?"

If you make cleaning up a family routine, like brushing teeth, your child is bound to start doing it on his own. If you enjoying picking up and organizing, then your child will adopt a positive, no-hassle attitude about being tidy.

PICKY EATING

All parents want their children to develop healthy eating habits. Wouldn't it be great if your child ate everything you put in front of her? Basically, if you buy the right food and prepare it in healthful ways, your kid will eat. However, a four- to seven-year-old's refusal to eat may actually have less to do with the food and more to do with the need to engage in something more exciting than eating. Unfortunately, at this age playing trumps mealtime.

Children don't eat when they're not hungry. If your child isn't hungry, don't try to make her eat. Children are natural grazers, so make only healthy foods available. There's no need to obsess over your picky eater, because most often young children consume the right amount and type of food to meet their nutritional needs.

The fast and busy pace of a child's world may leave him not at all interested in eating a full meal—let alone sitting down with the entire family. Toddlers have unbounded energy and little focus, so don't expect them to sit still for a family meal or at a restaurant. Four- and five-year-olds are at the perfect age to start learning to sit and socialize with others while they eat. Teach your child that food is yummy and that mealtimes can be fun and rewarding.

Never force your child to eat. Don't let your child's eating habits become an arena for a power struggle. Don't beg, bribe, or threaten, or offer to make something else for your child to eat. Explain that this is the meal being served, but be sure to include something he likes in the meal, in case he chooses not to try everything.

The following are some other tips.

1. Be a good food role model.

Research has shown that parents who are picky eaters tend to have children with similar traits. Children see their parents as role models and will mimic how they eat. I don't like certain sauces on my food, and wouldn't you guess it, neither do my kids! But I do try to eat a broad variety of good food. (If you have a secret cookie stash, be sure it's high enough so they don't find it.) Let your child know that when you were little you didn't like certain foods either, but eventually you started eating different things. Never talk about dieting in front of your child. Talk about exercising, eating healthy foods, and not stuffing yourself when you're not hungry.

2. Make food look interesting and fun.

Use cookie cutters to make sandwiches into different shapes. Make a meal look like animals or cars. When we cook pancakes, we make them look like a teddy bear's head. We also make food sculptures with toothpicks, grapes, apples, raisins, or whatever will stack up shish-kebab style.

At the market, children can help load food in the cart or help pick out fruits and veggies. Invite your child to help prepare the meal or snack. My kids like to cut, so I give them a plastic knife and have them slice watermelon—it's safe and easy.

3. Try the "one-bite rule" or the "yuck or yum" tactic.

Many kids are afraid to try new things, so just ask them to try the food instead of insisting they eat it all. If they're totally opposed and you feel a power struggle surfacing, do the "yuck or yum" test. They take one bite and tell you if it's a yucky or a yummy. Don't ever force a child to eat. Once my husband insisted our son eat his cauliflower, and my son threw up. Some foods just don't appeal to kids—or adults, for that matter.

4. Limit sweets.

If you are set on offering a dessert after dinner, consider getting your child accustomed to eating yogurt, cereal, fruit, or applesauce. Never choose sweets as a regular offering. You should look at cookies and candies as special treats that are not part of regular healthy eating.

5. "Debrief" your kids about their friends' meals.

Do your kids eat better at someone else's house? Mine do. Have your child tell you what her friends eat and ask which of her friends' meals you could make for her.

6. Make super smoothies.

If your child eats very little food and you feel she's not getting proper nutrition, try making a fruit smoothie packed with vitamins and minerals. Ask the doctor which supplements are appropriate for your child and make a delicious concoction!

If your child is losing weight or completely refuses foods or liquids, consult with your pediatrician.

THE "GIMMES"

"Mommy, can we get this? I want it! I don't have this! Pretty please?" Sound familiar? Saying no to your child is never easy, but you can set the boundaries without being seen as the mean mommy or daddy.

It's okay to say no because you're the parent, but you must offer an explanation of your reasoning—your child deserves one, just as would any other person with whom you disagree. With adults, you normally, out of respect, offer an explanation. Without the explanation you're just practicing old-school parenting and not allowing your child to feel understood. Your answer should be consistent with your other behaviors. (If your child sees you giving in to impulse buys, you can't expect to be heard when you expound on the benefits of restraint!) When your four- to seven-year-old demands a pack of gum in the checkout line, let her know you don't have enough money with you for treats, but you'll consider it next time. As long as you respond honestly and genuinely, your children will understand (at least eventually).

If your child continues to nag, you can empathize by saying, "I know you love gum—so do I. We need milk and bread more than gum right now, so can you help me out and put that back?"

In our family, my husband is the big spender with the kids. When they're in line at the grocery store, he'll buy them gum if they ask for some. But me, I've never bought my kids candy at the grocery store; they'll ask, but I always respond with the same explanation: "We buy healthy food at the store. Candy is for special occasions." I use my nonnegotiating voice, and it seems to do the trick.

Once you've said no, stick to it—even if your child fusses or has tantrums. My favorite tactic when my son "oohs and ahhs" over a new toy is to say, "What a cool toy! I see you really love it; let's add that to your birthday or Christmas list." Works every time.

No parent wants to be considered the bad guy, so make sure your relationship is open and that you can be flexible if the situation warrants it. If we've had a great healthy lunch and the boys ask for some treats, I do let them indulge. Sometimes my son calls me the "No monster"—which makes me take a look at how many times I actually say no to him on a daily basis. Be sure you spend a lot of quality time with your children so that they don't become demanding. Have family fun time and make efforts to be lighthearted and silly. Play with your child and set healthy boundaries so that she'll feel that your bond is based on trust, not just on the yeses and nos.

NEW BABY

How you tell your child that a baby is on the way will depend on her age. If you tell a child under two years old, she'll look you in eye and then walk away. You can try giving her a baby doll to practice being a big sibling. If your child is four to seven, or older, she may very well ask how you got the baby in your tummy and how it will get out.

When I became pregnant with my second son, my older son was four—so I was able to have a fairly realistic conversation with him. I had a hard time getting pregnant the second time, and every now and then my son would ask, "Am I ever going to have a sister or brother?"

I'd look at him in amazement, as I wondered that myself. My appropriate mommy response was, "We have to pick the right star from the sky that will be our baby." Each night from then on, my son would run outside with Daddy and pretend to grab a star, run back inside, and push his hand onto my tummy.

One morning, when I finally made it to nine weeks of pregnancy, my son said, "Mommy! There must be a baby in your belly because it's really big now." I smiled but didn't want to tell him until we got to the safe twelve-week zone. I said, "Let's hope so! With all those stars you picked, one of them must have worked! Let's wait two more weeks to see if your star grows."

Two weeks later we gave him the happy news, "I knew that!" he said, "I just knew there was a real baby in there." Hmm . . . he did know, and we couldn't keep it from him; he was too excited about getting his new sibling. We depended on him for his support and enthusiasm for the next six months.

As we neared the baby's birth date, our son asked how the baby would get out. There are two ways, I told him: one way was through my tummy; the other way was through the baby passageway near where I go pee. He was worried that both those ways might hurt, so he recommended I poop it out.

Choose a Style You Feel Comfortable With

Each family has their own set of morals and values and may decide to tell their child the scientific truth, or to take a whimsical approach as we did. There really is no one "right" way to break the news. However, preparing your child is key, so at some point your firstborn needs to know that she'll be sharing Mommy and Daddy with a new sibling.

Making your child your little helper and telling him that you'll be sleeping more and nursing baby often will be prepare him for the adjustment. We'd ask our son, "What do you think our new baby will do for the first few months?" He would say, "Cry, cry, cry." He got that right!

The day I gave birth, we gave our five-year-old a wrapped gift and told him it was from his star, his new little brother. He played with that toy truck for three hours in my recovery room. It was the second best day of my life.

THE GO-TO MOM'S QUICK AND NIFTY TIPS

Let Kids Play with (This) Food!

Have your child finger-paint with pudding and let him eat it afterwards. Use a sheet of waxed paper as the base and plop down a heap of chocolate pudding. He can also use big marshmallows as paintbrushes. What kid wouldn't love to eat his masterpiece?

Combat Nightmares with Bedtime Buddies

If your child develops a fear of the dark, have her place a few of her stuffed animals at the end of her bed. Call them "bedtime buddies" and tell her that these buddies will protect her at night. Your child can place an animal at her bedroom door as well.

Try the Good-Dream Box to Ensure a Good Night's Sleep

Offer the good-dream box and the bad-dream box to ease your child's mind of nighttime fears. Use your hands as the good-dream box: cup your hands together to form a box and have your child open it, pull out all the good dreams, and sprinkle them around his bed. Then cup your hands to make the bad-dream box—have him put his bad dreams in the box and then toss it out. Your child will have a night filled with lovely dreams.

Have Fun with the Tooth Fairy

How much do you leave—a dime, a quarter, or ten dollars? It's not the amount of money that children look forward to—it's the mystery and magic of the tooth fairy. When the tooth fairy visits, she comes with the intention of welcoming your child into the world of big-kid teeth. A quarter or a gold dollar is whimsical enough.

The fact that she leaves a cool trinket, which in the past has traditionally been money, really excites kids. Have you ever had a creative tooth fairy visit your child? She left two polished Sacagawea dollar coins and a few shiny crystals for our son.

No need to go overboard and leave paper dollars. Young children thrive on fantasy, not monetary items, and a few shiny quarters will surely bring a twinkle to their eye.

6

Unconditional Parenting

The One Job You Can't Quit

> We must be willing to feel uncomfortable if we are to
> turn the corner from denial to exuberance.
>
> —Naomi Aldort

The other day, I was walking through the parking lot of Target and saw a beautiful little girl in a yellow sundress lying on the grease-spotted ground next to her mom's SUV, crying her eyes out. Her mother squatted next to her, gently consoling her. I smiled because this was the essence of real parenting: *compassion*, whenever and wherever our children need it.

Fifteen minutes later, I left the store with 4T underwear in one hand and cat food in the other. I could see the SUV was still there, and I figured they must be inside the car trying to regroup. As I passed, I nonchalantly peered in the back window, and to my surprise I saw the mom holding her four-year-old in her lap in the back hatch area.

This mom was doing whatever it took to accommodate her little girl, and that's how parenting should be. Sometimes life's about sitting in your car while holding your distressed child.

There are many days when I'd like to throw in the towel— my kids can send me over the edge. I find myself yelling and threatening. How can that be? After all, I am the Parenting Expert. But even parenting experts recognize the challenges of being a parent. Anyone entering parenthood does so with her unique perspective, ideals, and personal baggage. I have to admit that the weight of my own baggage is what drew me into a helping profession. For years I've battled with the fact that my parents had children when they clearly didn't want to—leaving my siblings and me feeling like inconveniences. I wish I could claim I wrote this book because I had a warm and loving upbringing—but I didn't. This quote from Marshall B. Rosenberg describes the way most parents feel:

> Every time we're less than perfect, we're going to
> blame ourselves and attack ourselves; our children
> are not going to benefit from that. So the goal I
> would suggest is not to be perfect parents but to
> become progressively less stupid parents—by
> learning from each time that we're not able to give
> our children the quality of understanding that they
> need, that we're not able to express ourselves
> honestly.

I try to undo the damage and sift through the mixed messages and self-doubt that were the result of my parents' naïveté. No parent intentionally sets out to do harm. I honestly believe my parents only did what they knew, which was to do the bare minimum to raise their kids, without seeking any help or educating themselves about child rearing. They weren't perfect, and I don't expect to be perfect myself. I look at the upside of my childhood and consider it a lesson learned—or a trauma that has morphed into a gift—that I can offer to parents. I'm not trying to sound like a martyr, but for me to understand and move past my disarrayed childhood, I have to see the luminous light at the end of the tunnel.

As my boys grew, I promised myself to break the cycle of gen-erational old-school parenting. I wouldn't hit, scream at, or belittle my children. I thought nature would prevent me from having difficult children because I deserved a second chance and would have the ideal family. I quickly learned how naïve and innocent I was, because I still find myself slipping into dysfunctional parenting habits at times.

I try hard to be a good parent. If you don't try hard to be good at the things you love, then you'll never excel at them. If you don't make efforts to be a good parent, then you won't be one. Parents have the toughest job. I admire that mom in the Target parking lot. She's an amazing mother—and trust me, her children know that. Do your kids know that about you?

KNOW YOUR HOT BUTTONS

If as a child you had to earn your parents' love and acceptance, you may feel that your children need to earn yours. When your temper flares up because of something your child is doing, the experience may just be a terrible reminder of times when you felt no one was there for you—or you may feel that because you wouldn't dare misbehave in front of your parents, your children need to behave for you.

When our spouse, partner, or children push one of our hot buttons, it's easy to become angry and react impulsively, to be set off into an irrational outburst that can lead us to become a coercive parent. I know—I've been there myself! No one wants to look like a buffoon in front of his or her kids, but once they push that button, it's easy to spiral out of control. We justify being defensive when we give in to our anger, and take it out on our children, which is never productive or healthy.

Pick your battles and know that nothing is so important that it warrants extreme anger and coerciveness with your child. Being honest with your child is more effective than hauling off on her. I remember cooking dinner one night and the boys wouldn't listen; I was tired, hot, and overwhelmed. I got so upset that I lost control and threw a dish in the sink and yelled at them. In a flash I was completely ashamed and acutely aware that I had done the wrong thing. I knew I had scared them, but that hadn't been my intention—I was just irate. I apologized and asked my boys to be more helpful.

Children who are raised in homes where empathy is the norm are usually empathic toward their parents. It's not my sons' job to forgive me, but it is my job to apologize and show them that no one is perfect, not even Mommy. I ask the boys to help me out and make efforts to listen more when Daddy is not home because they know that being a mom is hard work. I'm tickled by this quote from my older son: "Moms are supposed to be frustrated—they don't need to always be happy, and that is okay."

Things to Do Instead of Getting Outwardly Angry and Scary!

- Walk away and take a deep breath. Remind yourself that this shall pass. Return to your kids and start over.
- Ask yourself what your mother or father would have done. Was it helpful or hurtful?
- Ask yourself if your kids are driving you crazy because they're just being kids or because they really are engaged in something inappropriate or dangerous.
- Is your hot button being pushed because your kids are behaving in a way that your parents would never allow when you were a child?
- Look inside yourself and see if it's just one of those days when a helping hand would really take the edge off being a parent. Pick up the phone and ask a friend to help.
- If you lash out and unravel, don't avoid the issue or act as if it never happened—this only teaches children to deny their own poor behavior. Apologize and show your children that they're worth the effort.

ACKNOWLEDGE YOUR PAST

You can be a better parent if you make an effort to recall memories from your past. It can be easy to recall the fond memories of childhood, but not the negative ones. Can you remember the bad messages you were given, the scary moments where you felt alone, or the confusing adult behaviors you were exposed to? As a parent you'll be at a disadvantage if you can't recall those emotional times or acknowledge painful memories. Unresolved issues from our past drive our current beliefs and behaviors.

Getting rid of negative early childhood messages is a start. Were you told that you were lazy, weren't trying hard enough, needed to buck up, or should speak only when spoken to? Were you expected to hug Aunt Tonia when she felt like a stranger to you? Were you forced to play on the volleyball team because your dad insisted you were a great athlete? Were you the youngest child who always got the leftover cold bathwater? You may unwittingly carry many situations from your past into your current parenting practices.

One mother told me she never bought her daughter toys because she didn't have them when she was little. I asked her how old her daughter was, and she said two. I perked up! "This is the perfect time for social play!" I said, and explained how children at that age love to play with toy farms and pretend animals, dolls, and pots and pans. I encouraged her to find toys that supported her child's developmental stage.

She got a horse and barn play set for her daughter, and later called to thank me. She said her daughter played for hours on end with the new toys. After a few days of watching her daughter play with the horse and barn, this mom became flooded with early childhood memories. She told me about her sadness over never being able to play the way her daughter was. Money wasn't the issue, she said; her parents just never gave her toys. My heart went out to her as we talked about the other parts of her childhood that left her feeling deprived.

SEPARATE YOURSELF FROM YOUR CHILD

I see many of my own traits in my children, and it's these very traits that create intense emotions in me. I'm very headstrong and assertive. When my son puts his foot down or outright defies me, I feel my blood pressure rise.

The old cliché "It takes one to know one" is grounded in truth. When I turn to my husband for guidance and tell him that our son is being stubborn and strong willed, he teases me and says, "I wonder where he got that from?" Well, I've got the will of a one-ton bull—if I believe in something, I won't budge until a tractor comes to push me out of the way. I've passed that trait on to my sons, and I am left feeling helpless when they hold their ground.

Let Your Kids Be Themselves

I've learned to honor my boys' temperaments and to keep my anger in check. I choose to discuss how I feel when I see shadows of my personality in them. When I was young and my parents saw their traits in me, I was punished. They didn't have the knowledge or ability to empathize or recognize that parents pass traits down to their kids. When children are old enough to discuss these feelings, it helps to clear the air so that you can go back to creating a loving and kind environment. When my kids don't eat, I tell them that when I was little I didn't want to eat some of the meals my mom made either. I also tell them that I was forced to eat, which made me mad. I ask them if they'd be willing to eat what they can so that they don't go to bed hungry. The honest and supportive dialogue always brings us closer.

Your children no doubt have traits that you don't possess, and that's not so bad! My son has an amazing ability to apologize very easily—which I greatly admire. In contrast, I am highly guarded and self-conscious, and have great difficulty saying "I'm sorry" to other adults. I'm amazed when I see my children excelling in areas where I still struggle.

Sometimes I find myself wishing that my oldest son were more social, like my husband and me. On a scale of 1 to 10, with 10 being highly comfortable initiating conversation with others, I'm a 10+. My son is a 2. I try my hardest not to impose my desire on him. Yes, it would be great to see him mingle and be more confident, but his temperament is set, and I have to respect him for that. Plain and simple: we're not our children, and they're not us. Trying to make our children be more like us won't make them better people.

You'll find that you may enjoy certain stages of parenting more than others. It's okay to reminisce and miss the times that have passed with your child. It's also normal to excitedly await a future stage if the one you're in now with your child is difficult for you. I love the baby stage because I can give unlimited amounts of love without the fear of rejection. When children get older, they can choose to reject you when they feel inclined to do so. My girlfriend couldn't bear the baby stage; she said all the dependence and crying was hard for her. She loves the preschool age, when she can have conversations with her daughter.

Embrace your child as she grows into her own person. I'm pleased my kids want to camp in the cold mountains, whereas I'd rather be covered in honey and swarmed by ants! Even though I personally don't like being dirty, I have a mud pit in my backyard so that my boys can experience the joy of being dirty—an experience that I never had.

Give your child freedom to make choices for themselves. If my son is outdoors and isn't cold, I don't insist he wear a jacket; how do I know what his internal body temperature is? I have poor circulation, so I need a sweater outdoors, but why should I impose my body issues on him? If I'm chilled and put on my long-sleeved pajamas, I don't make my son wear his; I let him choose what is comfortable for him. This kind of flexibility teaches children to appreciate that everyone is different.

When we honor our children, they in turn honor us. I find it endearing that on our family movie night my son tells his dad,

"Mommy doesn't like dramas or action films; she'll only watch funny movies, so pick a funny one!"—no judgment or begging and pleading to change the movie to his preferred show, just acceptance of how Mom's choice of entertainment is different.

If children learn to trust themselves, they learn to face disappointment with strength and resiliency. If there's no one to blame, they learn to take on personal responsibility. When a child is efficient with self-expression and knows that his parents accept his unique character, he can take on life with confidence and vigor. Accepting your children for who they are is one of the best gifts you can give them. Children who are respected and emotion coached know right from wrong and can be incredibly resourceful.

Keep Adult Issues out of Your Child's World

Children don't deal with their emotions the same way adults do. For the most part, grown-ups are articulate, intentional, and rational. We have to be good listeners with our children no matter how they choose to express themselves. They won't meet us at our level of communication or understand how the world works until they are older. At no point should children be expected to hear about grown-up issues or problems. I don't disclose scary or harmful stories from my childhood to my kids, nor do I discuss within my children's hearing any details of the last R-rated movie I went to see. They're too young to understand. Sharing adult information or asking a child to be overly mature is parentifying her—treating her like a friend or another adult. Kids don't need to know about adult issues, especially painful ones. Children are empathic by nature and will take on your stress and try to help heal your past wounds, but that's not your children's job.

Sharing your past if fine, as long as it doesn't push your child into a caretaking role. There are clearly certain times when you need to discuss some adult issues with your children—for example, when a loved one passes away, loses a job, gets divorced, or has a serious illness. Otherwise, keep adult conversations, issues, and concerns out of your child's world.

Emotion Coach Your Spouse or Partner

Parents who emotion coach each other are more likely to have happier children than families who don't. When we connect to our partner, keep the conflict mild, and reach an appropriate resolution, we set the stage for healthy human interaction. When you're empathic toward your spouse, your child sees the value in taking care of the people he loves. Disagreeing in a respectful way in front of your kids helps them see how two people can be at odds but still love and care for one another. Your child will also see that you say no to others and not just to them!

Building a strong emotional bond with your spouse is good for everyone. It makes your marriage more cohesive and offers your kids the opportunity to be more socially intelligent. Look around, and you can see that socially bright children have better tools for fending off youth violence, bullying, drug addiction, teen pregnancy, suicide, and criminality.

DIVORCE AND SINGLE PARENTING

In a perfect world, divorces would be amicable, and all family members would fare just fine. But the truth is, divorce can be quite traumatizing for both parents and children. Whether you are married, separated, or divorced, if you are critical of and contemptuous with your partner, your child is more likely to be aggressive and to have problems getting along with others. Children who are raised in the midst of a nasty or heated divorce have been found to have elevated stress hormones, problems soothing themselves, and increased health problems. Children who are exposed to constant hostility or avoidance-posturing—one parent trying to alienate the other—during a divorce will have serious emotional issues.

Five-year-old Lillian's parents divorced, and a year later her father remarried. Lillian is put in an awkward position because her father and stepmom won't allow her mom to come into their home to see Lillian's new room. Lillian automatically goes into a caretaking role with her mom when she gets picked up: she feels sorry for her mother because her father won't address the issue of why Mommy is not allowed in his house. It might ease Lillian's anxiety and sadness if both parents emotion coached her about how hard it must be to have two separate families.

Kids feel they have to take sides to make sense of their parents' divorce. They'll either side with the weaker parent if they feel that the parent can't cope alone, or will join the angry or wronged parent by rejecting the other. If you're going through a divorce or separation, don't put your child in situations that may interfere with her long-term emotional development.

Parents who are going through a divorce are often preoccupied, stressed, and unsupportive of their children. This leaves kids at risk for being exposed to harsh or inconsistent discipline. When adults are too busy fighting battles, they spend very little quality time with their children. Children in this situation may drift, cut themselves off from their painful emotions, or join risky peer groups to make up for the lack of connection at home.

Regardless of how you feel about your ex-partner, let your child know how much you loved the other parent. Take the high road—you're shaping your child's view of how love and relationships should be. Explain that you were no longer getting along and that living away from each other was the best way to stay friends. Let your child explore his emotions. Children sometimes have fantasies that their parents might someday get back together (except in cases of domestic violence). Be open to the expressions and hopes that your child shares with you. Even if your child blames you, hear him out—because in his world someone is to blame, and it's better that he targets you than himself, which in most cases children do.

Enrique's mom is an emotion coach; she encourages all her children to express themselves and to come to her when they need help. Enrique's parents have been divorced for eight years. When Enrique turned nine, he asked his mom why she and his dad got divorced. He even went so far as to ask her if she still loved his dad. She explained to him that they were no longer friends and that the arguing was making them very sad. She said that when they divorced they became better friends. She wanted to avoid putting Enrique in a position where he might take sides, so even though she no longer loved her ex-husband, she told Enrique that she did. She wants her children to know that relationships can work and that love is an integral part of them no matter what the end result may be.

Emotion coaching kids through a divorce is the ideal thing to do. However, the disturbing truth is that children who come from divorce can become alienated from one parent when they grow up. This is concern enough to take divorce very seriously and tread carefully when children are involved. Just because you and your ex-partner have a fractured relationship doesn't mean that you and child should. Emotion-coached kids fare very well when both parents take the time to accommodate their children's emotions. Emotion coaching serves as a protective agent when couples are not getting along or have to divorce. It's crucial that parents remain emotion coaches to their children regardless if they choose to stay in a conflictual marriage or go ahead and call it quits.

When to Introduce the Person You're Dating to Your Child

There are no hard-and-fast rules on when a single parent should introduce a new partner to her child. Here are some things to consider:

- Keep your dating life separate from your family life until you know this is going to be a long-term relationship. And keep appropriate boundaries during the dating process to protect your little one from attaching to someone who may not be looking for a long-term commitment. It is not the specific amount of time that has passed but the nature of the commitment that evolves between you and a future partner that should determine when he meets your child.

- When you do introduce a potential partner, start off slowly with limited activities like going to the park or the zoo.

- Wait until there is a clear commitment to the relationship—or potential for marriage—before assigning parental tasks to your new partner.

- When sufficient time has passed and you know this person is in for the long haul, introduce him to your child as a "new friend."

- Be honest with your child. Set boundaries and don't encourage her to see your date as her new parent. Children don't know what dating is, and they don't need a detailed explanation—just telling them Lynn is your good friend is explanation enough.

Children need time to adjust to the reality that Mommy or Daddy needs friends too, so give lots of love and support to them when you decide to introduce your future partner.

MAKE TIME FOR YOURSELF

Just because you have kids doesn't mean you can't carve out time for your personal well-being. Parents who take time to tend to their own mental health are more present for their children. It's one of the hardest things to do, but it's of the utmost importance. Here are some ideas.

Make efforts to engage in what I think of as self-cherishing activities. How many times this month have you done something just for yourself? Did you take a nice long bubble bath, read a book, or watch your favorite team play football? Parents are happier and more mentally balanced when they engage in activities that fuel their passion for life. When you run an errand, tack on an extra half hour to do something fun. I know parents think they don't have a spare second to grab a vanilla iced-blended coffee or to flip through the pages of a cool magazine at the bookstore, but why not? We deserve it.

As I mentioned in Chapter Three, another great way to hold on to your sanity is to ask for—or pay for—help whenever possible. Yes, you'll have to overcome your "I can do it all" mentality, but to be the happiest and most effective parent you can be, you need to allow yourself the breathing room that others can offer.

Stressed-out parents are not fully present with their children. Simplify your life by doing less or cutting out what's not necessary. Doing nothing or being alone can be immensely valuable. Never underestimate the power of decompression time for Mommy and Daddy. Just as sleeping serves to restore our mind and body, doing nothing can do the same for parents. It's okay to have nothing on your plate! The most common advice I give parents is to cut out what is not absolutely necessary. Simplify. Less is more.

Learn to take grown-up time-outs when you're angry or cranky. My family and I are all better off when I announce, "Mommy needs a time-out!" than when I take my stress out on the family— which is what can happen when I don't take a break. I don't mean that you should take a break and sit down for minute—I'm talking about taking several hours off of parenthood to do something that brings back your vitality.

Quiet yourself at least once a day. There are very few moments of stillness when you're raising kids. Taking time for yourself is essential for good parenting. If we don't take care of ourselves, we will eventually burn out or lash out at our loved ones. Taking time off from chores, work, and family can be very grounding.

Date Your Partner or Spouse

It's easy to fall into the family trap where kids are number one and most of your energy is directed at taking care of your children and maintaining family harmony. But remember this: family harmony is best sustained when Mom and Dad share a fondness for one another the way they did when they were first dating.

Yes, it takes time, effort, and a little planning to rekindle the ol' spark. Moms and dads need to take time away from the kids to reconnect. At first it may feel as though you're just going through the motions, but once you get out and realize you're on a real date, you'll have a wonderful time.

Many couples don't make dinner reservations once they've had kids, but that doesn't mean that your spouse won't take you out at the drop of a hat if he knows that's what you want. Even if your date consists of just eating hot dogs or taking a trip to the beach, I'm sure he'll do most anything to ensure a night of closeness—which is rare when you're raising kids. If your other half doesn't know you like to be wined and dined or adored and pampered before you get intimate, then tell him.

What Men Said a Perfect Date Night Would Look Like

Cocktails at sunset on an outside patio somewhere downtown, a nice dinner, and music at the Continental Club.

—Brad, Texas

An evening where my wife can let her guard down and act like the woman that I dated before we had kids. Drinks, dinner, and the opportunity to talk honestly about our lives.

—Matt, California

Horseback ride at Spur Cross Reserve with chilled margaritas and a sunset picnic.

—Scott, Arizona

After a three-day stay at a hotel on the beach, rise and shine to some hot coffee and muffins from the lobby. Enjoy some morning smooching and whatever may happen next. . . . Stroll to a nearby café for a nice leisurely breakfast and check out, depart for airport and flight home to our baby girl (first class seats).

—Larry, California

More than one night, preferably over 300 miles away . . . like Las Vegas. But for one night: an evening at an expensive dinner with a bottle of wine, and possibly a movie or play.

—Ryan, California

A great dinner and a few hours in a movie theater. Just to get away from it all. My wife, on the other hand, finds movies a waste, as we aren't really "spending the time engaged" together, talking and such. I of course disagree and find that we can do that during dinner, and the movie allows us both a mental escape and some rare time together when we have no stress of life intruding.

—Doug, California

A nice quiet evening at home with lots of sex!

—Paul, Colorado

Dinner by the beach followed by a walk along the shore.

—Adrian, California

Don't use your children as an excuse to avoid getting out and becoming reacquainted with your partner. Personally, I'm hesitant to go to distracting movies, games, or concerts because they don't lend themselves to strengthening my relationship with my husband. If you and your spouse date frequently, then it's fine to go on outings where you don't interact. If you've been married for a long time and actually prefer not to talk to your spouse, I hope you have other ways to connect.

My husband and I both work and take care of our boys. We have to make a point to set up date nights, or we'd never see each other. I've been married for twelve years and still look forward to date night. And believe it or not, my husband has never set up a single one! I always do it. Moms usually hold the family calendar and know just when it's the best time to leave the babes behind.

If I left date night up to my husband, he'd probably plan it at the last minute, make the reservations very late, and spend way too much money. Now, I like to be taken out to nice restaurants, but I'm also fine with just laughing and catching up while eating tacos or pizza. No need to go into dinner debt! So he does appreciate that I take the initiative to make plans.

My older son used to love having a babysitter, but lately he says that he's sad when we go on dates. The other night he told me that he misses us and wishes that we'd never leave for a date. Well lucky me, I let him watch NickJr's *Little Bill* that day, and lo and behold, the show was about how Little Bill's parents needed some time alone. I thought, *Someone is watching out for me!* I felt for a moment that TV isn't that senseless after all.

Far too often, I hear moms say that they don't date their spouse because they have very little time. I ask, Do you have time for sex? Most say yes. We all know that a quickie encounter is awesome and sometimes all we have time for, but don't kid yourself. Couples are more likely to enjoy the closeness if they can go on an official date—sans the kids.

THE GO-TO MOM'S QUICK AND NIFTY TIPS

The Happy Hour Date

Budgets are tight these days, so going out to a nice restaurant isn't always an option. But that doesn't mean you can't go out and have a terrific time. There are dozens of places that offer inexpensive drinks and food at happy hour.

You're probably thinking, "Okay, I'm married with kids, and you're suggesting happy hour?" Just because you're married with kids doesn't mean you can't party the way you used to! So get online and Google nearby restaurants to see who offers a happy hour.

The Love Map Date

My all-time favorite marriage pick-me-up book is *Seven Principles for Making Marriage Work*, by John Gottman. This book is a fantastic guide to help couples have a harmonious and long-lasting relationship. I've read this book multiple times during my marriage to keep my cohabiting skills sharp, and I whip it out whenever I notice tension or distance between my husband and me. Sometimes I even leave it on my hubby's dresser or in the bathroom in hopes that he'll give it a read.

However, what usually happens is that he'll ask, "The marriage book is out; are we okay?"

The book has a Love Map Questionnaire that you can bring with you on a date to add some laughter and fun. Although the quiz is designed to be taken with a pen and paper, I like to just bring it along and take turns asking the questions. There's also a "fondness and admiration" questionnaire to determine the degree of fondness between you and your partner. Gottman's work is by no means intended to shake up your marriage, but he sure does have some amazing exercises that will humble any individual who is married.

If your relationship needs mending—more attention and loving care—I highly recommend the book *Fighting for Your Marriage: Positive Steps for Preventing Divorce and Preserving a Lasting Love*, which helps spouses hear each other and be heard and offers practical strategies for resolving conflict.

Common Questions from Go-To Mom Viewers

In this chapter I offer ideas, tips, and guidelines in response to the questions I hear most from parents all over the country who watch the Go-To Mom shows. The shows I've produced have been inspired from my viewers' questions.

WHY DOES MY CHILD CLING?

My twenty-six-month-old has been extremely clingy lately. He cries every time I leave the room—even to take a shower. I'm not sure if it is because of his age or our new baby.

This is normal behavior for children under three, and you're correct to make a connection that the presence of your new baby may be the culprit. Children your son's age are gaining independence and practicing separation from Mommy; however, even though they are more adventurous, they may become more needy emotionally. Independence is a simple concept for an adult to understand, but a scary one for a child.

You'll find your son becoming particularly clingy when you do things for yourself—brushing your teeth, cooking, or making a phone call. He senses your independence and is afraid you won't return. Whether you're going to the bathroom or actually leaving the house on an errand, he feels the same emotional sting. Now that you have a new baby, he probably feels the shift in your energy, and his clinginess kicks into high gear.

Things to Help Your Child Feel More Secure

- Be sure he has an attachment object like a blankie or stuffed animal to soothe himself in your absence.
- When you intend to take a shower, tell him ten minutes in advance; let him know he can play with special toys while you're showering.
- When he cries or shows fear, say, "It's hard for you when Mommy is busy—you just want to be with me! I love you too."
- Sometimes all it takes is for you to stop what you're doing, give a loving hug, and read him a book.
- Make him your little helper when tending to your baby.
- Join a playgroup or set up regular play dates with children who are close in age. Toddlers need to play with their peers; it's an essential part of teaching socialization.

There's nothing you can do to prevent this natural developmental phase. Most toddlers find it distressing to be separated from people they love. Although it looks as though your child is miserable during your absence, there's no actual harm done to him. Look at separations as opportunities to renew your bond when you get back.

WHY DOES MY CHILD RESIST GETTING DRESSED EACH DAY?

I don't blame kids for not wanting to get dressed—I love spending the day in my PJs too! Children like predictability, so they sometimes resist getting dressed because their pajamas are a reminder of the comfort of home. Children frequently view getting dressed as a chore.

Ways to Encourage Your Child to Get Dressed

- Creating a routine is the key. Have your child get dressed first thing in the morning. Get him on a regular routine of getting dressed and going outside to transition him slowly out of this PJs-home comfort zone.
- Make getting dressed fun. Create a game out of it or sing a song!
- You can let your child wear her jammies longer at night to get her in the mind-set for bed; however, don't let her hang out in them all morning.
- Talk about the importance of needing to get dressed and that everyone gets dressed—let him know that you will let him play in his cozy jammies at night.
- Empathize with her feelings and let her know that you miss her during the day when she's at preschool and that you look forward to evenings when everyone gets in his or her jammies.

If your child resists leaving home in the morning, it may be an indication that he needs more time with you. Being home makes him feel that connection.

HOW CAN I HAVE A NO-GIFT BIRTHDAY PARTY FOR MY CHILD?

I suggested to my partner that we shouldn't have presents at Melanie's (turning four) birthday party. Our family will give her gifts separately. But we will ask her friends not to bring gifts because we want Melanie to focus on the celebration and her friends and not on the "stuff" that comes with parties.

It's common for parents to feel that their children have too many toys. Sometimes, however, the more you focus on that, the more your child will want. Once we tug, our children will tug back. I recommend a relaxed approach about receiving gifts. This "no-gifts" concept is really part of an adult philosophy, not a child's issue. Your child may wonder about or be saddened by the fact that other children receive gifts for their birthday—why isn't she?

If you're concerned that your daughter may become over-indulged or greedy, having a no-gift birthday won't teach her thankfulness. My children love toys and are very lucky that their grandparents and I buy them. If my son becomes unappreciative, I gently remind him that he has a lot of toys, and I ask which toys he'd like to give away so he can make room for the new ones. He usually ends up saying, "I don't need new toys; I want to keep these, Mama!" Now that my son is older, he's more willing to fill a bag with toys to give to less fortunate children so that he can make room for the new ones.

If you're set on having no gifts and your child is genuinely fine with that, then on the invitations you can state "No gifts, please" or "No gifts, please, but if you're inclined to do so, books are appreciated." That way if a guest chooses to bring a gift, she won't feel guilty about violating your request. If people bring gifts, place them in a back room and have your daughter open them when everyone leaves. If you take a relaxed approach, then everyone wins. The gift-givers feel appreciated, and the child gets something special. There really are no rules, but you don't want to offend guests who like to bring gifts. Teach flexibility by being flexible yourself.

IS THERE EVER A TIME WHEN A LIGHT SWAT IS OKAY?

Children learn best through positive experiences; it's never okay to swat or hit them. If you strike a child, the only lesson learned is that people with power always get their way. Children may misuse power and imitate your methods to gain power themselves, whether it's with a sibling, pet, or friend.

When a child is hit, his brain shuts down to protect himself, causing him to retreat mentally—it's therefore unlikely that he'll learn a lesson. Parents usually spank out of anger and truly believe that it's all they can do to stop their child from misbehaving. If you can recall your own childhood, do you remember how it felt to be hit or spanked? It was no doubt belittling and humiliating, and you probably only stopped your behavior out of fear of another spanking—or fear of having your parents reject you. If your parents had given you a choice either of being hit or being spoken to, which would you have chosen? Give your child a chance—and break the cycle of aggressive parenting practices.

Our kids will benefit the most if we guide them by setting limits, giving them love, and teaching them reason and logic. All it takes is a commitment to being the type of parent you'd like to be and to creating the type of world you'd want your child to live, love, and grow in.

ARE WE BEING OVERPROTECTIVE?

My husband is very protective, and I feel he's not letting our daughter live her life, not letting her grow up the way we did. Is he doing any harm? She's five, and he still thinks she'll choke on toy pieces, and if a child has a runny nose at a birthday party, he rushes her home.

Parents who have a strong need to hyperparent or to control their child's environment usually have some unmet need that makes them feel helpless and out of control. Your husband's tendency to overprotect and shield your daughter from the world may be a way of regaining control that he lost in his past.

Hyperparenting can have some pretty serious repercussions. When children are shielded from every aspect of life, they never learn to be responsible for themselves; they become overly reliant on others and have a hard time trusting their own instincts. They may see the world as an unsafe place to live. When we hover, the message our children receive is, "You're not capable." Children are *very* capable and deserve the right to live securely in this world.

Parents need to protect their children, but at some point they also need to give them breathing room for healthy growth. Kids usually don't need heightened supervision after the age of four. It's no longer protection but paranoia when a parent continues to treat his preschooler as if she were a baby. Children learn about the world and how it works from their parents. If you see the world as a diseased and unsafe place, so will your child. This only leaves her at a disadvantage when she becomes an adult.

SHOULD MY CHILD BE LEARNING THE ABCs AND HIS NUMBERS BEFORE KINDERGARTEN?

Research shows that children under five years of age don't need formal academic instruction to be ready for school. In fact, loving homes where the parents often play and have frequent conversations with their kids have children who do well in kindergarten. The best indicator that a child will be a good reader and writer is if the parents read to him and make books available at home. Your child is more likely to love reading if your home has books scattered around for him to pick up and explore. If you read, he'll read.

A young child's brain and muscles are still in an early stage of development, and it is neither healthy nor productive to push the acquisition of academic skills. We risk killing a child's spirit and stripping him of his innate love of learning when we impose formal academic instruction too early. By the time a child turns five, she begins to show interest in using a pencil and paper. School serves to enhance children's naturally occurring skills and helps them read and write more quickly.

I never taught my son how to hold a pencil or crayon. He didn't even like pencils. After his first week in kindergarten, he came home and began to write letters using a pencil. I was happy to see that we had done the right thing by not pushing any formal instruction. The closest we came to "real" teaching was playing with ABC magnets on the fridge, singing the ABCs, and pointing at and labeling pictures in books; mostly, though, we gave our son lots of love and attention. That's all kids really need to be ready for school.

What Kindergarten Teachers Really Want

Contrary to popular conceptions of what it means for a 5-year-old to be ready for kindergarten, most kindergarten teachers are not wishing for rooms full of children who can already identify the letters of the alphabet. Instead what they want are children who have learned how to regulate their impulses, follow through on a difficult task and have the self-control to listen to the teacher's directions for a few minutes.

—Early Ed Watch Blog, 2009

Schools are created to teach children how to read and write. Teachers get their credentials to teach children these skills. Parents can support and guide. Give yourself a break and let your child play outside, sing, build, create, paint, experiment with glue and strings, laugh, and get really dirty.

MY FOUR-YEAR-OLD CHILD IS MEAN TO OUR DOG. IS THIS NORMAL?

Very young children don't know how to handle family pets appropriately; they need to be guided on how to gently touch, care for, and show respect to them. Many children lie on animals or pull and tug on them because they're not aware that animals have feelings and experience pain just as we do. You should model caring behavior and remove your child if he's being cruel to your pet. It is never okay to let your child hurt a pet. Teach him to talk to your dog by using caring and loving words like "We love you, Rocket. You're fun to touch and soft to pet." And reinforce to your child that "We never hurt our dog; it makes him sad."

Children who are bullied or picked on may take their frustration out on family pets or on wildlife (insects, bugs, and so on). One of the ways a child works through trauma or recoups his power is to hurt things that are smaller and more helpless than he. Sometimes abusing pets or animals can be a sign of mental illness. If this is a recurring issue in your family, take your child to see a family counselor.

HOW DO I HANDLE IT WHEN MY PRESCHOOLER IS MAD AND TELLS ME, "I DON'T LOVE YOU" OR "I HATE YOU, MOMMY!"

Hate is a pretty strong word, and I encourage families never to use it. Instead encourage your child to say "I don't like you." Children who feel safe at home and with their parents may say things like this, which is good; it means they feel safe enough to express themselves without fearing you'll abandon them. When you allow your child to vent, she'll be more likely to let you know how she's really feeling and why she's distraught. When my son tells me he wants a new mommy, I say, "What did I do? You know I love you." It opens the dialogue for him to let me know what's going on.

Emotion-coached kids don't stay mad for long. Once they've been heard, they go back to appropriate forms of expression. If your child says hurtful things to you, go through the steps of emotion coaching (Chapter Two) to see what the deeper issue may be.

AT WHAT POINT IS YELLING ABUSIVE? I YELL AT MY KIDS, BUT THEY DON'T LISTEN OTHERWISE

All parents yell at some point or another. Some yell "Dinner's ready!" or "Get off of your sister; she's not a chair!" But at what point is yelling damaging to your child's development? It's not the yelling per se; loud voices generally don't traumatize children. However, a scary tone or threatening message is pretty much all a kid needs to see that you have lost composure and self-control.

An emotion coach doesn't resort to that type of communication. Parents are not perfect, and when we're stressed we're at risk for yelling at the ones we love. Children model our behaviors, so if you find yourself screaming at your kids, catch yourself and regroup. Let your child know that when you're frustrated you sometimes yell, and that this is not good. Fess up and apologize. Tell her you need her help and cooperation.

Never yell as a scare tactic; it's cruel, and the image of you terrifying your child may be imprinted in her mind forever.

MY HUSBAND AND I ARE ON TWO DIFFERENT PAGES WHEN WE PARENT. SHOULDN'T WE BE USING THE SAME DISCIPLINE PHILOSOPHY?

No one is perfect, so don't sweat the small differences between your style and your partner's. It's the big issues (punishing, using time-outs, using consequences, and so on) that really require both parents to be in sync. It's common for one parent to rely on techniques that may actually reinforce poor behavior while the other focuses on correcting it in a way that's too severe. It's okay if Dad lets the kids play longer at the park than Mom or if he gives more milk at dinner. But when it comes to discipline, both parents should be in agreement over core beliefs about how their kids should be treated. Parents need to discuss strategies that typically don't work—for example, blaming, shaming, punishing, or minimizing—and educate themselves on what does work. Parents should discuss the idea that effective discipline typically doesn't involve any punishment, but instead should teach their child what to do or what's expected.

It's very important that parents don't criticize and judge one another (especially in front of the kids). Partners who don't insult each other and who compromise tend to be on the same page most of the time.

Make a cheat-sheet and refer to it when times get tough and you're not sure what do to. My husband likes to remind himself that consequences should always fit the behavior. If our son throws his die-cast cars, we ask him whether what he's doing is okay, then we brainstorm solutions with him so that he doesn't throw them again. If he continues to throw, we take the cars away, as opposed to holding back dessert that evening, which is not related to the misbehavior.

You can create a signal that one or both of you use when things go off course. If one of us slips and threatens our boys, we calmly say "old school" into the other's ear to remind us that what we're doing isn't effective, and we can immediately correct our stance. Keep the lines of communication open with your partner and appreciate your differences. Emotion coach your partner and talk about why he or she is relying on ineffective tactics. It's also helpful to take a parenting class or read the same parenting books together so that you can become more of a team.

WHEN DO I TEACH PERSONAL SAFETY? I DON'T WANT TO PUT BAD IDEAS IN MY KID'S HEAD IF I DON'T HAVE TO

Real responsibility that ensures a very young child's safety lies with the parents or caregivers. Children can't be responsible for their personal safety until they are older. This doesn't mean that you can't begin to teach your child some basics. Discuss personal safety with your child in an open manner so that if something comes up, she'll talk to you.

Children are better prepared to protect themselves when taught appropriate safety concepts that aren't based on fear. Inducing fear doesn't empower kids—doing so scares them and can leave them feeling helpless. The more involved you are in your child's life, the less likely it is that your child will seek attention from other adults.

Here are some safety issues you can discuss with children who are between the ages of three and five years:

1. *Your body is your own.* Tell them, "Only Mommy, Daddy, and the doctor can touch your private areas." Define private parts. Teach them to say, "No, I don't like that" and to tell you right away if someone touches their body in way that they don't like. This needs to be an ongoing discussion to reinforce the concept.

2. *Running away or wandering off from an adult is not okay when in public.* Let your children know that running away from you or any other grown-up they're with is dangerous—because they can get lost, and grown-ups are not allowed to be separated from their children in public.

3. *Standing up for yourself is okay.* Encourage your children to say no and to stand up for themselves if anyone hurts or scares them, and make sure they know that they should always tell you. Emphasize that parents are here to help and protect their kids.

Here are some more safety issues to add to the list as your child gets older:

1. *Always check with us or other trusted adults before going anywhere.* It's never okay to go anywhere without permission from you.

Give your children a list of the adults who can pick them up from school. Go over the list and the rules on an ongoing basis.

2. *Tell us or other trusted adults if anything bad happens to you or if something makes you feel sacred, confused, or in danger.*

3. *No one has the right to force, trick, or pressure you into doing things you don't want to do.*

I regularly discuss safety issues with my eight-year-old, as he's no longer in my care during the day. When we send children off to school, we do so under the assumption that teachers and grownups typically do the right thing—which in some cases is not true. If I didn't have these discussions with him, I wouldn't know about the inappropriate things that go on at school. I'm not so naïve to believe that all teachers and administrators behave appropriately. I've walked the schoolyard and have seen for myself how some grown-ups treat kids—which is all the more reason to encourage your child to come to you when they have a feeling or notion that something's wrong.

I started having serious discussions with my son when he entered kindergarten. I'm thankful that he's comfortable telling me things because I would never be privy to what happens if he didn't. When he was a kindergartener, he told me that his teacher gave time-outs to kids who didn't listen. I figured in a class that big, that's probably the only thing that worked for her. But when he came home and said she gave him a time-out, I said, "Were you not listening?" He told me that he had been crying and had been held inside from recess because he forgot his homework.

Yes, I had to stay composed, because my top was about to blow! How can a five-year-old remember his homework when he can barely remember to get dressed?! Five-year-olds are not even technically in grade school yet—not to mention that she was using an ineffective strategy by trying to motivate him negatively.

If I didn't have that open relationship with my son, he would have been put in time-outs all year round. Talk with your kids and, most important, stand up for them!

MY DAUGHTER IS ONLY IN FIRST GRADE AND IS EXPOSED TO BULLIES. WHAT CAN WE DO?

It's important to take bullying very seriously and to recognize that it has a terrible effect on the lives of kids. Bullying happens when someone purposefully scares or hurts another a person. It's not surprising that kids as young as five show bullying behavior. Usually bullying happens repeatedly, and as kids get older, it can turn into cyber-bullying once they have access to computers and cell phones.

Older kids who are bullied are more likely to skip school, have low self-esteem, smoke, drink alcohol, and take drugs. Bullying should not be taken lightly. The Columbine kids, Dillon Klebold and Eric Harris, were continually bullied, and we all saw the effect it had on them. Yes, there were clearly other contributing factors that led those boys to commit their unspeakable act, but Klebold and Harris were known to be picked on by cliques in their school and regularly bullied. This itself is enough for all schools to have a "zero tolerance" policy on bullying and violence.

Because bullying threatens children's safety and emotional health, we need to teach kids about compassion and responsibility. Parents need to be their child's number one advocate because most adults and teachers don't see bullying when it happens. Kids who feel unsupported are afraid to report bullying.

When your child tells you that kids are being mean to her, empathize with her and let her vent how she feels. Once you've heard her side, ask her if the both of you can go speak to her teacher or to the principal. Explain that bullying should not be ignored, because if it goes ignored, then the bully will hurt others. Remind her that it is your job as a parent to protect her.

It's also important that you find out what your child's school policy is on bullying. Never minimize or deny your child's experience if she tells you that someone is treating her poorly. Take a stand and give a helping hand.

For more information or to watch webisodes that empower kids on how to understand and stop bullying, go to www. StopBullyingNow.hrsa.gov.

HOW CAN I PROTECT MY CHILD FROM TOXIC FOOD AND ENVIRONMENTS AND HELP HIM REDUCE HIS CARBON FOOTPRINT AND WASTE PRODUCTION?

Everyone wants her children to breathe healthy air, drink safe water, and be protected from toxins and sun exposure. It's not as overwhelming as one may think to convert to a healthier lifestyle. My husband and I have been slowly "greening" our house and taking environmental issues to heart. It really starts before your child's birth—having to protect a child in utero so that she can be strong enough to live in today's world.

When we brought our first precious bundle of joy home from the hospital, I immediately began to worry because we live in a 1920s craftsman home. I was aware that old paint contained lead. I asked my father if he thought we should strip all the windowsill paint and apply a fresh coat to get rid of the potential lead.

"You don't need to strip down old paint," he said, "unless you think your kid is going to eat the windows."

Well, twelve months later when my son began to walk, his favorite thing to chew on were the windowsills because they were at level with his mouth! The reality is that kids will eat whatever they want that's in arm's reach until they get old enough to know better.

A few years after I had my boys, news hit about the dangers of a toxic chemical, bisphenol A (BPA), which was found in baby bottles and in the linings of formula cans. Today we also know that it's in most canned foods! I was shocked and dismayed because after I nursed I used bottles and formula with both my sons. Research found that in some cases, a single serving of canned food was enough to expose a woman or infant to BPA levels that were two hundred times higher than what the government considered safe for industrial chemicals. This was enough for me to make a lifestyle change to ensure a safer life for our boys.

Quote from an Activist

Nobody can do everything but everybody can do something.
—Gil Scott-Heron

Years ago, if you were an organic activist, you could wind up being viewed as a tree hugger or a "granola" person. Times have changed, and being green is increasingly viewed as a civic duty. The things my family did to live a more eco-friendly life took only a few weeks to implement. Educate yourself on harmful ingredients and then read the labels before you buy, switch out your household cleaners and lightbulbs, or buy organic foods—you don't have to do it all at once. If we can do it, so can you—aren't your kids worth it?

Here are some practical tips if you want to move from hazardous to healthy:

- Reduce exposure to phthalates, the industrial compounds added to increase the flexibility of plastics, by avoiding polyvinyl chloride (PVC) and purchasing products from companies that have eliminated phthalates. When burned, PVC plastic releases dioxins—a group of the most potent synthetic chemicals ever tested, which can cause cancer and harm the immune and reproductive systems. In studies on people, boys born to mothers with greater exposure to phthalates had altered genital development. Phthalates may also cause asthma as well as liver and kidney damage.

- Stop heating plastic containers and plastic wrap in the microwave—use glass containers to heat food. Heating plastic can cause BPA in the plastic to migrate into food.

- Say good-bye to fragrances—buy all-natural and unscented products. Some air fresheners, candles, detergents, shampoos, and perfumes contain phthalates (plasticizers).

- Look on the bottom of plastic containers and bottles, and stay away from anything with the symbols 3, 6, and 7—these are the dangerous plastics.

- Store food in glass containers or safe plastic containers—buy plastic wrap and bags made from polyethylene, which doesn't have plasticizers.

- Toss out the PVC toys. Choose wooden toys (unpainted) and cloth and plush toys. Soft toys that you can squeeze are commonly made of vinyl and PVC. Toy companies that have stopped using PVC include Sassy, Tiny Love, Early Start, Little Tikes, Lego, Prime Time Playthings, Brio, Chicco, Evenflo, First Years, and Gerber.

- Use silicon nipples and pacifiers.

- Get a lead testing kit to check old chipping paint, toys, cups, lunch boxes, and so on for lead.

- Check to see if any of your child's art products have been recalled; certain crayons, chalk, and craft pieces have been recalled by the Consumer Product Safety Commission due to high levels of lead.

- Stay away from foods that contain high levels of pesticides. Whenever possible, try to find organic varieties of the following produce: peaches, apples, sweet bell peppers, nectarines, strawberries, cherries, lettuce, grapes, pears, spinach, and potatoes. Nonorganic varieties are usually cultivated using high amounts of pesticides.

- Buy nitrate-free preserved meats—stay away from bacon, hot dogs, and lunchmeat if nitrates are listed on the label. You can usually find nitrate-free meats in most grocery stores, or ask the store manager to stock them.

- Avoid canned foods. BPA is found only in processed, manufactured foods and packaging. Eat fresh, raw produce whenever you can.

- Compost fruit and vegetable waste. Williams-Sonoma, for example, has a great countertop stainless-steel compost container that you can dump your shavings and coffee grounds into. If you have a garden, you can start a pile outdoors. Or give your compost to someone who has one.

- Use fluorescent lightbulbs instead of incandescents. Some cities will give you free lightbulbs for your entire house.

- Ditch the Teflon. Teflon releases a chemical that can cause cancer. Use stainless steel, copper-coated, or cast-iron cookware.

- Buy Energy Star appliances to reduce energy consumption.

- Toss out toxic skin care products—soaps, lotions, sunscreen, and makeup. Go to Safecosmetics.org to get a list of healthy alternatives for you and your children.

- Keep keys away from kids; some contain lead.

- Get a HEPA filter if you have family members who have allergies or asthma.

- Reduce, reuse, recycle—let's hope that this is the norm for all of us by now!

- Stop using plastic bags. Tote food home from the grocery store in your own canvas bags.

- Use stainless steel water bottles instead of disposable plastic bottles—this is better both for your health and for the environment.

- Send your child to school with an eco-friendly lunch bag. If you do a Google search for "organic and eco-friendly kid's lunch bags," you'll be surprised just how many companies offer them. Instead of using plastic sandwich bags in your child's lunch, switch to reusable food containers.

- Avoid toxic household cleaners.

For more information on how to make your child's world a safer place, visit HealthyChild.org, Healthytoys.org, EPA.org, Safecosmetics.org, EWG.org, and Cosmeticsdatabase.com.

THE GO-TO MOM'S QUICK AND NIFTY TIPS

Make Homemade Healthy Play Dough

One cup of flour

One cup of water

Half a cup of salt

Two tablespoons of oil

Two tablespoons of cream of tartar

If you want to color the dough, either add food coloring to the water or, to make the dough more organic, use beet juice, spinach juice, or carrot juice as directed below.

Mix the flour, salt, and oil in a large bowl, then slowly stir in the water. Place in a pot and cook over medium heat, stirring until the dough becomes thickened and ball-like. This takes only a minute or two; don't let it overcook or burn! Remove the dough and place it on a sheet of wax paper, kneading it with your hands. Form it into three balls and add a few drops of the vegetable juices to each ball, then knead that in and begin to play. Store the play dough in an airtight container in the fridge, and it should last up to one year!

EPILOGUE

I hope this book will be helpful when you have a parenting question about what to do with your child's emotions and behavior today, tonight, next week, next month, and in the years to come.

Whatever wisdom there is in this book comes from my years of teaching and clinical counseling with parents who have told me what's worked for them, and from my own experience as a mother.

I've learned, sometimes by making mistakes, that the best way to understand a child's world is to put yourself in her shoes. The basis of good parenting is empathy, love, and the deep meaning of the relationship with your child.

It's always possible to learn more, polish our skills, and improve our parenting style. It's never too late to strengthen the bond with our children. We want our children to be successful in everything they do. Lend a loving hand, be a gentle guide, and, most important, take your child's emotions seriously. When the teen years approach, you'll see all your hard work pay off.

Please write to me with your own comments, feelings, and advice at info@thegotomom.com, and stop by my Web site, TheGoToMom.TV, a place where parents can learn to be great role models for their children. The two-minute video segments are easy for you to view anytime, anywhere.

REFERENCES

Aldort, N. (2006). *Raising our children, raising ourselves: Transforming parent-child relationships from reaction and struggle to freedom, power and joy.* Bothell, WA: Naomi Aldort, PhD (Book Publishers Network).

Cohen, L. J. (2002). *Playful parenting.* New York: Ballantine Books.

Coronato, H. (2008). *Eco-friendly families: Guide your family to greener living with activities that engage and inspire . . . from toddlers to teens.* New York: Alpha.

Dombro, A., & Lerner, C. (2005). *Bringing up baby: Three steps to making good decisions in your child's first years.* Washington, DC: Zero to Three.

Dreikurs, R., & Soltz, V. (1980). *Children: The challenge:* New York: Plume.

Dutwin, D. (2008). *Unplug your kids: A parent's guide to raising happy, active, and well-adjusted children in the digital age.* Cincinnati, OH: Adams Media.

Faber, A., & Mazlish, E. (1995). *How to talk so kids will listen and listen so kids will talk.* New York: Harper Paperbacks.

Garbarino, J., & Bedard, C. (2001). *Parents under siege: Why you are the solution, not the problem, in your child's life.* New York: Free Press.

Gavigan, C. (2008). *Healthy child healthy world.* New York: Dutton.

Ginott, H., & Ginott, A. (2003). *Between parent and child: The best-selling classic that revolutionized parent-child communication* (Rev. ed.). New York: Three Rivers Press.

Gottman, J. (1998). *Raising an emotionally intelligent child: The heart of parenting.* New York: Simon & Schuster.

Gottman, J., & Gottman, J. S. (2003). *And baby makes three: The six-step plan for preserving marital intimacy and rekindling romance after baby arrives.* New York: Three Rivers Press.

Grille, R. (2005). *Parenting for a peaceful world.* New South Wales, Australia: Longueville Media.

Hart, S., & Hodson, V. K. (2006). *Respectful parents, respectful kids: 7 keys to turn family conflicts into cooperation.* Encinitas, CA: Puddledancer Press.

Heim, S., & Engel-Smothers, H. (2008). *Boosting your baby's brain power.* Scottsdale, AZ: Great Potential Press.

Hirsh-Pasek, K., & Golinkoff, R. M. (2003). *Einstein never used flash cards: How our children really learn and why they need to play more and memorize less.* Emmaus, PA: Rodale Books.

Holinger, P. (2003). *What babies say before they can talk: The nine signals infants use to express their feelings.* New York: Fireside.

Holt, J. C. (1995). *How children learn.* New York: Da Capo Press.

Hunter, A., & Walker, J. (2007). *The Moms on Call guide to basic baby care: The first 6 months.* Grand Rapids, MI: Revell.

Hyman, I. (1997). *The case against spanking: How to discipline your child without hitting.* San Francisco: Jossey-Bass.

Kashtan, I. (2005). *Parenting from your heart: Sharing the gifts of compassion, connection and choice.* Encinitas, CA: Puddledancer Press.

Kohn, A. (2005). *Unconditional parenting: Moving from rewards and punishments to love and reason.* New York: Atria.

Kurcinka, M. S. (2001). *Kids, parents and power struggles.* New York: Harper Paperbacks.

Kurcinka, M. S. (2007). *Sleepless in America: Is your child misbehaving or missing sleep?* New York: Harper Paperbacks.

Kvols, K. J. (1998). *Redirecting children's behavior*. Seattle: Parenting Press.

Lieberman, A. F. (1995). *The emotional life of the toddler*. New York: Free Press.

Markman, H., Stanley, S., & Blumberg, S. (2001). *Fighting for your marriage: Positive steps for preventing divorce and preserving divorce and preserving a lasting love*. San Francisco: Jossey-Bass.

Melmed, M. (1997, July). Parents speak: Zero to Three's findings from research on parents' views of early childhood development. Public policy report. *Young Children, 52*(5), 46–49.

Miller, A. (2002). *For your own good: Hidden cruelty in child-rearing and the roots of violence* (3rd ed.). New York: Farrar, Straus and Giroux.

Perry, B. D. (1994). Neurobiological sequelae of childhood trauma: Post traumatic stress disorders in children. In M. Murburg (Ed.), *Catecholamine function in post traumatic stress disorder: Emerging concepts* (pp. 253–276). Washington, DC: American Psychiatric Press.

Riak, J. (2009). *Plain talk about spanking*. Parents and Teachers Against Violence in Education.

Rosenberg, M. (2003). *Nonviolent communication: A language of life* (2nd ed.). Encinitas, CA: Puddledancer Press.

Runkel, H. E. (2008). *Screamfree parenting: The revolutionary approach to raising your kids by keeping your cool*. New York: Broadway Books.

Schickedanz, J. (1999). *Much more than the ABCs: The early stages of reading and writing*. Washington, DC: National Association for the Education of Young Children.

Siegel, D., & Hartzell, M. (2001). *Parenting from the inside out: How a deeper understanding can help you raise children who thrive*. New York: Tarcher.

Sobel, D. (1999). *Beyond ecophobia: Reclaiming the heart in nature education.* Great Barrington, MA: Orion Society.

Straus, M. A. (1999, October 5). Is it time to ban corporal punishment of children? *Journal of the Canadian Medical Association, 161,* 821.

Swallow, W. K. (2000). *The shy child: Helping children triumph over shyness.* New York: Grand Central Publishing.

Teicher, M. H. (2002, March). Scars that won't heal: The neurobiology of child abuse. *Scientific American, 286*(3), 68–75.

Wesselman, D. (1998). *The whole parent: How to become a terrific parent even if you didn't have one.* New York: Da Capo Press.

THE GO-TO MOM'S "BEST BOOK" CORNER

Books for Parents

Aldort, N., *Raising Our Children, Raising Ourselves: Transforming Parent-Child Relationships from Reaction and Struggle to Freedom, Power and Joy* (2006)

Cohen, L. J., *Playful Parenting* (2002)

Coronato, H., *Eco-Friendly Families: Guide Your Family to Greener Living with Activities That Engage and Inspire . . . from Toddlers to Teens* (2008)

Dreikurs, R., and Soltz, V., *Children: the Challenge* (1980)

Dutwin, D., *Unplug Your Kids: A Parent's Guide to Raising Happy, Active, and Well-Adjusted Children in the Digital Age* (2008)

Faber, A., and Mazlish, E., *How to Talk So Kids Will Listen and Listen So Kids Will Talk* (1995)

Garbarino, J., and Bedard, C. *Parents Under Siege: Why You Are the Solution, Not the Problem, in Your Child's Life* (2001)

Ginott, H. G., *Between Parent and Child: The Bestselling Classic That Revolutionized Parent-Child Communication* (2003)

Gottman, J., *Raising an Emotionally Intelligent Child: The Heart of Parenting* (1998)

Gottman, J., and Gottman, J. S., *And Baby Makes Three* (2007)

Gottman, J., and Silver, N., *The Seven Principles for Making Marriage Work* (1999)

Children's book lists courtesy of the Center on the Social and Emotional Foundations for Early Learning (CSEFEL)

Gurian, M., *The Purpose of Boys: Helping Our Sons Find Meaning, Significance, and Direction in Their Lives* (2009)

Hart, S., and Hodson, V. K., *Respectful Parents, Respectful Kids: 7 Keys to Turn Family Conflicts into Cooperation* (2006)

Heim, S., and Engel-Smothers, H., *Boosting Your Baby's Brain Power* (2008)

Hirsh-Pasek, K., and Golinkoff, R. M., *Einstein Never Used Flash Cards: How Our Children Really Learn and Why They Need to Play More and Memorize Less* (2003)

Holinger, P., *What Babies Say Before They Can Talk: The Nine Signals Infants Use to Express Their Feelings* (2003)

Holt, J. C., *How Children Learn* (1995)

Kashtan, I., *Parenting from Your Heart: Sharing the Gifts of Compassion, Connection, and Choice* (2004)

Kohn, A., *Unconditional Parenting: Moving from Rewards and Punishments to Love and Reason* (2005)

Kurcinka, M. S., *Kids, Parents, and Power Struggles* (2001)

Kurcinka, M. S., *Sleepless in America: Is Your Child Misbehaving . . . or Missing Sleep?* (2007)

Kvols, K. J., *Redirecting Children's Behavior* (1998)

Lerner, C., and Dombro, A. L., *Bringing Up Baby: Three Steps to Making Good Decisions in Your Child's First Years* (2005)

Markman, H., Stanley, S., and Blumberg, S., *Fighting for Your Marriage: Positive Steps for Preventing Divorce and Preserving a Lasting Love* (2001)

Pieper, M. H., and Pieper, W. J., *Smart Love: The Compassionate Alternative to Discipline That Will Make You a Better Parent and Your Child a Better Person* (1999)

Pipher, M., *Reviving Ophelia: Saving the Selves of Adolescent Girls* (1995)

Rosenberg, M. B., *Nonviolent Communication* (2003)

Runkel, H. E., *Screamfree Parenting: The Revolutionary Approach to Raising Your Kids by Keeping Your Cool* (2008)

Schickedanz, J. A., *Much More Than the ABCs: The Early Stages of Reading and Writing* (1999)

Siegel, D., and Hartzell, M., *Parenting from the Inside Out: How a Deeper Understanding Can Help You Raise Children Who Thrive* (2001)

Sobel, D., *Beyond Ecophobia: Reclaiming the Heart in Nature Education* (1996)

Swallow, W. K., *The Shy Child: Helping Children Triumph over Shyness* (2000)

Wesselman, D., *The Whole Parent: How to Become a Terrific Parent Even If You Didn't Have One* (1998)

Kid Books About Feelings

ABC Look at Me! by Roberta Grobel Intrater (infant–4)

"Baby Faces" books (most are by Roberta Grobel Intrater) (infant–4)

Big Feelings: A Book Filled with Emotions, Talaris Institute (2009)

Can You Tell How Someone Feels? by Nita Everly (3–6)

Double-Dip Feelings, by Barbara S. Cain (5–8)

The Feelings Book, by Todd Parr (3–8)

Glad Monster, Sad Monster, by Ed Emberley and Anne Miranda (infant–5)

The Grouchy Ladybug, by Eric Carle (1–6)

Happy and Sad, Grouchy and Glad, by Constance Allen (4–7)

How Are You Peeling: Foods with Moods/Vegetal Como Eres: Alimentos con Sentimientos, by Saxton Freymann (5–8)

How Do I Feel? by Norma Simon (2–7)

How Do I Feel?/Como Me Siento? ed. by the editors of the American Heritage Dictionaries (infant–4)

I Am Happy, by Steve Light (3–6)

If You're Happy and You Know It! by Jane Cabrera (3–6)

Little Teddy Bear's Happy Face, Sad Face, by Lynn Offerman (a first book about feelings)

Lizzy's Ups and Downs, by Jessica Harper (3–9)

My Many Colored Days, by Dr. Seuss (3–8)

On Monday When It Rained, by Cherryl Kachenmeister (3–8)

Proud of Our Feelings, by Lindsay Leghorn (4–8)

See How I Feel, by Julie Aigner-Clark (infant–4)

Sometimes I Feel Like a Storm Cloud, by Lezlie Evans (4–8)

Today I Feel Silly and Other Moods That Make My Day, by Jamie Lee Curtis (3–8)

The Way I Feel, by Janan Cain (3–8)

What I Look Like When I Am Confused/Como Me Veo Cuando Estoy Confundido, by Joanne Randolph (5–8)

What Makes Me Happy? by Catherine and Laurence Anholt (3–6)

Kid Books on Sad Feelings

Franklin's Bad Day, by Paulette Bourgeois and Brenda Clark (5–8)

Hurty Feelings, by Helen Lester (5–8)

Knuffle Bunny, by Mo Willems (3–6)

Let's Talk About Feeling Sad, by Joy Wilt Berry (3–5)

Smudge's Grumpy Day, by Miriam Moss (3–8)

Sometimes I Feel Awful, by Joan Singleton Prestine (5–8)

The Very Lonely Firefly, by Eric Carle (4–7)

When I Feel Sad, by Cornelia Maude Spelman (5–7)

Kid Books on Angry or Mad Feelings

Alexander and the Terrible, Horrible, No Good, Very Bad Day, by Judith Viorst (4–8)

Andrew's Angry Words, by Dorothea Lackner (4–8)

Bootsie Barker Bites, by Barbara Bottner (4–8)

The Chocolate-Covered-Cookie Tantrum, by Deborah Blementhal (5–8)

How I Feel Angry, by Marcia Leonard (infant–4)

How I Feel Frustrated, by Marcia Leonard (3–8)

Lily's Purple Plastic Purse, by Kevin Henkes (4–8)
The Rain Came Down, by David Shannon (4–8)
Sometimes I'm Bombaloo, by Rachel Vail (3–8)
That Makes Me Mad! by Steven Kroll (4–8)
The Three Grumpies, by Tamra Wight (4–8)
When I Feel Angry, by Cornelia Maude Spelman (5–7)
When I'm Angry, by Jane Aaron (3–7)
When Sophie Gets Angry—Really, Really Angry, by Molly Garrett (3–7)

Kid Books on Scared or Worried Feelings

Creepy Things Are Scaring Me, by Jerome and Jarrett Pumphrey (4–8)
Franklin in the Dark, by Paulette Bourgeois and Brenda Clark (5–8)
I Am Not Going to School Today, by Robie H. Harris (4–8)
No Such Thing, by Jackie French Koller (5–8)
Sam's First Day (in multiple languages), by David Mills and Lizzie Finlay (3–7)
Sheila Rae, the Brave, by Kevin Henkes (5–8)
Wemberly Worried, by Kevin Henkes (5–8)
When I Feel Scared, by Cornelia Maude Spelman (5–7)

Kid Books on Self-Confidence

ABC, I Like Me, by Nancy Carlson (4–6)
Amazing Grace, by Mary Hoffman (4–8)
Arthur's Nose, by Marc Brown (3–8)
The Blue Ribbon Day, by Katie Couric (4–8)
I Am Responsible! by David Parker (3–5)
I Can Do It Myself, by Emily Perl Kingsley (2–4)
I'm in Charge of Me! by David Parker (3–5)
The Little Engine That Could, by Watty Piper (3–7)
Susan Laughs, by Jeanne Willis (4–7)

Too Loud Lily, by Sophia Laguna (4–7)
Try and Stick with It, by Cheri Meiners (4–8)
26 Big Things Little Hands Can Do, by Coleen Paratore (1–6)
The Very Clumsy Click Beetle, by Eric Carle (3–7)
Whistle for Willie/Sebale a Willie, by Erza Jack Keats (4–7)
You Can Do It, Sam, by Amy Hest (2–6)

Kid Books on Behavior Expectations

Can You Listen with Your Eyes? by Nita Everly (6–7)
Can You Use a Good Voice? by Nita Everly (6–7)
David Gets in Trouble, by David Shannon (3–8)
David Goes to School, by David Shannon (3–8)
Excuse Me! A Little Book of Manners, by Karen Katz (infant–5)
Feet Are Not for Kicking (available in board book), by Elizabeth Verdick (2–4)
Hands Are Not for Hitting (available in board book), by Martine Agassi (2–8)
I Show Respect! by David Parker (3–5)
I Tell the Truth! by David Parker (3–5)
No Biting, by Karen Katz (infant–5)
No, David! by David Shannon (3–8)
No Hitting, by Karen Katz (infant–5)
Words Are Not for Hurting, by Elizabeth Verdick (3–6)

Kid Books on Family Relationships

Are You My Mother? by P. D. Eastman and Carlos Rivera (infant–5)
Baby Dance, by Ann Taylor (infant–4)
Counting Kisses, by Karen Katz (infant–5)
Don't Forget I Love You, by Miriam Moss (2–7)
Guess How Much I Love You, by Sam McBratney (infant–5)
Guji Guji, by Chih-Yuan Chen (5–8)

How Do I Love You? (available in board book) by P. K. Hallinan (infant–5)

I Love You: A Rebus Poem, by Jean Marzollo (1–6)

I Love You the Purplest, by Barbara M. Joose (4–8)

The Kissing Hand, by Audrey Penn (3–8)

Koala Lou, by Mem Fox (4–7)

Mama, Do You Love Me?/Me Quieres, Mama? by Barbara Joosse (3–6)

More, More, More, Said the Baby: Three Love Stories, by Vera B. Williams (infant–3)

Owl Babies, by Martin Waddell (3–7)

Please, Baby, Please, by Spike Lee (infant–5)

Te Amo Bebe, Little One, by Lisa Wheeler (infant–3)

You're All My Favorites, by Sam McBratney (5–7)

Kid Books on Problem Solving

Don't Let the Pigeon Drive the Bus! by Mo Willems (2–7)

Don't Let the Pigeon Stay Up Late! by Mo Willems (2–7)

I Did It, I'm Sorry, by Caralyn Buehner (5–8)

It Wasn't My Fault, by Helen Lester (4–7)

Talk and Work It Out, by Cheri Meiners (4–8)

Kid Books on Bullying and Teasing

The Berenstain Bears and the Bully, by Stan and Jan Berenstain (4–7)

Big Bad Bruce, by Bill Peet (4–8)

Chester's Way, by Kevin Henkes (5–7)

Coyote Raid in Cactus Canyon, by J. Arnosky (4–8)

Gobbles! by Ezra Jack Keats (4–8)

Hats, by Kevin Luthardt (3–6)

Hooway for Wodney Wat! by Helen Lester (5–8)

Hugo and the Bully Frogs, by Francesca Simon (3–7)

A Weekend with Wendell, by Kevin Henkes (4–8)

Kid Books on Grief and Death

The Fall of Freddie the Leaf, by Leo Buscaglia (5–adult)
Goodbye, Mousie, by Robi Harris (3–8)
I Miss You, by Pat Thomas (4–8)
The Next Place, by Warren Hanson (5–adult)
Sad Isn't Bad: A Good-Grief Guidebook for Kids Dealing with Loss, by Michaelene Mundy (5–8)

Positive Parenting Web Sites

Baby Center
www.babycenter.com

Building Blocks for a Healthy Future
www.bblocks.samhsa.gov

Center on the Social and Emotional Foundations for Early
    Learning (CSEFEL)
www.vanderbilt.edu/csefel/

Child Welfare Information Gateway
www.childwelfare.gov

Fussy Baby Network
www.fussybabynetwork.org

The International Network for Children and Families
    (INCAF)
www.incaf.com

National Association for the Education of Young Children
www.naeyc.org

Talaris Institute
www.Talaris.org

Zero to Three
www.zerotothree.org

Parent Training and Education

The Basics of Nonviolent Communication (Marshall Rosenberg)
www.nonviolentcommunication.com

Brazelton Touchpoints Center
www.touchpoints.org

Center for Nonviolent Education and Parenting
www.cnvep.org

The Gottman Institute (Strengthen and repair marriages and relationships)
www.gottman.com

The Incredible Years
www.incredibleyears.com

The International Network for Children and Families (INCAF)
www.incaf.com

Nurturing Parenting
www.nurturingparenting.com

Parent Effectiveness Training
www.gordontraining.com

The Parent's Toolshop: The Universal Blueprint for Building a Healthy Family
www.parentstoolshop.com

ABOUT THE AUTHOR

Kimberley Clayton Blaine is a mother, author, parenting expert, and licensed family and child therapist who specializes in working with children ages newborn to six years old. Kimberley is currently the social marketing director of Project ABC, a Los Angeles–based early childhood mental health campaign funded by the U.S. Department of Health and Human Services, SAMHSA Division.

Kimberley is the founder of the webshow www.TheGoToMom.TV. The Go-To Mom is a dynamic "how-to" online show for families with young children (newborn to age six). The Go-To Mom videos address such topics as parenting issues, discipline strategies, and emotion coaching.

Kimberley is an executive producer for Yahoo! and is a member of the Yahoo! Mother's Board of Bloggers. She lectures frequently and teaches courses in early childhood brain development and positive discipline strategies at UCLA Extension.

Kimberley is the creator of child abuse treatment activity books for the California Department of Criminal Justice Planning. Her latest publication for children is the *My Feelings Activity Book for Preschoolers*, created for Project ABC. She is the author of *The Internet Mommy, What Smart Mothers Know,* and *Mommy Confidence* (all published by CreateSpace). She frequently writes articles and blogs for traditional parenting magazines and Web sites.

You can contact Kimberley Clayton Blaine on twitter, @TheGoToMom; via e-mail, info@TheGoToMom.TV; or by visiting her Web site, www.TheGoToMom.TV.

INDEX

A

ABCs learning, 174–175
Adults: checking in with trusted, 179; running away from, 108–109, 179; school pick-up list of, 180; shielding your child from issues of, 158–159; teaching your child to ask for help from, 48, 76–77
Aldort, Naomi, 151
"All About Me" stage, 83–84
American Academy of Pediatric Dentistry (AAPD), 65
American Academy of Pediatrics (AAP), 59, 63
Anger: alternatives to expressing your, 154; child's hitting response to, 106–108; grown-up time-outs when feeling, 163; "I don't love you" or "I hate you" statements said in, 176; knowing your hot buttons leading to, 153–154; validating feelings of, 136; yelling out of, 136, 177. *See also* Emotions; Feelings
Animals: hurting, 176; keeping cats out of cribs, 79; teaching

caring behavior toward, 175–176
Apologies: role modeling, 130, 154; teaching your child about, 130
Assessing: child's behavior and triggers, 44–45; resolving power struggles by, 50–51; your child's needs, 45
Attachment objects: baby outings and use of, 70; blankets and stuffed animals, 61–63, 170; pacifiers, 63–65; separation anxiety and comfort of, 73
Attention: assessing and observing as paying, 44–45; babies and need for, 59–61; listening as paying, 45–46; motivating child with your, 22–23. *See also* Communication
Attention-seeking tantrums: dealing with, 102; description of, 101

B

Babbling, 60
Babies: accepting help with,

37–38; teaching your child appropriate, 37, 46. *See also* Communication; Crying

Emotional intelligence development, 2

Emotional Intelligence (Goleman), 2

Emotions: body-mind connection of, 47–48; empathy and support of child's, 10; healing process begun by verbalizing, 8; identifying and acknowledging your child's, 36–37, 46; learning to address your own, 11–12; separation anxiety, 72–74, 113, 127; set aside in order to feel empathy, 39–40; traumatized children's inability to express, 8. *See also* Anger; Fears; Feelings

Empathy: attention-seeking tantrums and, 102; bonding with your child through, 53; creating atmosphere of, 10; emotion coaching used to provide, 16; everyday practice of, 40–41; exploring child's statements and feelings using, 18–19, 39–40, 47; as foundation for effective parenting, 90; Go-To Mom bracelet reminder to practice, 40–41; using natural consequences along with, 24–25; providing

understanding and validation through, 23; setting aside your own emotions to feel, 39–40, 47; teaching your child, 20, 33–34, 61, 123

Empathy bracelet, 40–41

Energy Star appliances, 185

Environment: facilitating child's sleep by changing the, 120–121; nurturing and violence-free, 84; protecting your child from toxic, 182–186; research on children and predictability of, 59

Evidence-based parenting, 11

Excitatory phase, 55

Expectations: communicating to child your, 36–37; establishing age-appropriate, 82–83; unrealistic, 10, 28–30

External motivation, 21–23

F

Faber, Adele, 5

Family pets: keeping cats out of cribs, 79; teaching child caring behavior around, 175–176

Family rules: no hitting, 106–107; setting limits through, 82–83, 107

Fantasy tales, 138–139

Fathers: being open to emotion coaching, 14–15; perfect date night described by, 164–165

Fears: of clingy child, 169–170; common and changing,

New babies: different family
styles to prepare for, 148;
introducing older children to
idea of, 147
Nightmares: "bedtime buddies"
for combating, 148; good-
dream box to ease fear of, 149
Nighttime routines, 66–67
No-gift birthday party, 171–172
Numbers learning, 174–175
Nursing babies: during outings,
69, 70; during plane takeoff
and landing, 72

O

Observing: assessing your child's
needs by, 45; resolving power
struggles by, 50–51; your
child's behavior and triggers,
44–45
"One-bite rule," 144–145
Outdoor playing: getting dirty
during, 112; playground
etiquette for, 111–112
Outings. See Public outings
Overprotecting child, 173–174

P

Pacifiers: debate over using a, 63,
65; decreasing dependency
on, 64; securing by threading
hole of, 79
Parent-child interactions:
excitatory phase of, 55;
inhibitory phase of, 55–56.
See also Power struggles

Parent-child relationship:
behavior influenced by
strength of, 3; building
connections in your, 35–39;
focus on strengthening your, 5;
as heart of emotion coaching,
3–4, 35; playing with your
child to build, 37–38; "power-
with" type of, 10. See also
Children
Parenting: appreciating the
challenges of, 12; avoiding
negative, 26–31; breaking the
cycle of old-school, 152–153;
control-based, hands-off,
versus emotion control,
12–17; empathy as foundation
for effective, 90; evidence-
based, 11; learning art of
unconditional, 151–167;
single, 159–162. See also
Emotion coaching
Parenting for a Peaceful World
(Grille), 99
Parents: addressing their own
emotions, 11–12; confessing
mistakes, 51–53; conflict over
discipline approach by each,
177–178; discounting,
minimizing, and denying by,
17–21; divorce by, 159–161;
emotion coaching role of,
9–10; everyday practice of
empathy of, 40–41; helping
child cope with traveling,
127; know your hot buttons,

away behavior, 109; school performance and learning impaired by, 85; self-esteem destroyed by, 87–88; sending message that violence is okay, 85–87

"Spanking Strikes Out" (Poussaint), 85

Spoiling babies, 57–58

Spouses: dating your, 164–167; emotion coaching of your, 159; single parenting following divorce from, 159–162

Standing up for themselves, 179

Star Wars (film series), 132

Sticker rewards, 21–22

Strauss, Murray, 5

Stuffed animals: combating nightmares with "bedtime buddies," 148; encouraging sensitivity through interaction with, 123; using to gain cooperation, 103; separation anxiety and comfort of, 73; symbolism of, 61–63

Superhero play: description and concerns about, 132–133; healthy ways to support, 133–134

Swallow, Ward K., 137

T

Tantrums: avoiding power struggles over, 102–103;

dealing with attention-seeking, 102; description and types of, 101; handling public, 103–104

Teaching: appropriate emotional expression, 37, 46; babies to communicate their needs, 76; caring behavior toward family pets, 175–176; child to ask for help, 48, 76–77; child to depend on their feelings, 37; cleanliness, 142–143; the difference between lying and telling the truth, 139; empathy to babies, 61; empathy to your child, 20, 33–34; good manners and social grace, 129–130, 136; kindness and gratitude, 129; personal safety, 178–181; sensitivity to your child, 123; tooth care to preschoolers, 116–117; value of privacy, 129–130; your child to share, 109–111. *See also* Learning; Parents; Role modeling

Teaching conversations: on apologizing, 130; encouraging your child to get dressed, 171; to help your child feel more secure, 170; on a new baby in the family, 147; time-outs versus using reasonable, 23–24; on value of privacy, 129–130. *See also* Communication